CHEFMAN AIR FRYER COOKBOOK

TOP 250

Quick And Easy Budget Friendly Recipes
Fry, Bake, Grill, and Roast with Your
CHEFMAN Air Fryer

DEBORAH KINNEY

Copyright

Table of Contents

The Chefman air fryer is an easy way to cook delicious healthy meals. Rather than cooking the food in oil and hot fat that may affect your health, the machine uses rapid hot air to circulate around and cook meals. This allows the outside of your food to be crispy and also makes sure that the inside layers are cooked through.

Chefman air fryer allows us to cook almost everything and a lot of dishes. We can use the Chefman air fryer to cook Meat, vegetables, poultry, fruit, fish and a wide variety of desserts. It is possible to prepare your entire meals, starting from appetizers to main courses as well as desserts. Not to mention, Chefman air fryer also allows home made preserves or even delicious sweets and cakes.

How Does Chefman air fryer Works?
The technology of the Chefman air fryer is very simple. Fried foods get their crunchy texture because hot oil heats foods quickly and evenly on their surface. Oil is an excellent heat conductor, which helps with fast and simultaneous cooking across all of the ingredients. For decades cooks have used convection ovens to try to mimic the effects of frying or cooking the whole surface of the food. But the air never circulates quickly enough to achieve that delicious surface crisp we all love in fried foods.
With this mechanism, the air is circulated on high degrees, up to 200° C, to "air fry" any food such as fish, chicken or chips, etc. This technology has changed the whole idea of cooking by reducing the fat up to 80% compared to old-fashioned deep fat frying.

The Chefman air fryer cooking releases the heat through a heating element which cooks the food in a healthier and more appropriate way. There's also an exhaust fan right above the cooking chamber which provides the food required airflow. This way food is cooked with constant heated air. This leads to the same heating temperature reaching every single part of the food that is being cooked. So, this is only grill and the exhaust fan that is helping the Chefman air fryer to boost air at a constantly high speed in order to cook healthy food with less fat.

The internal pressure increases the temperature that will then be controlled by the exhaust system. Exhaust fan also releases filtered extra air to cook the food in a much healthier way. Chefman air fryer has no odor at all and it is absolutely harmless making it user and environment-friendly.

Benefits of the Chefman air fryer

- Healthier, oil-free meals
- It eliminates cooking odors through internal air filters
- Makes cleaning easier due to lack of oil grease

- Air Fryers are able to bake, grill, roast and fry providing more options
- A safer method of cooking compared to deep frying with exposed hot oil
- Has the ability to set and leave as most models and it includes a digital timer

The Chefman air fryer is an all-in-one that allows cooking to be easy and quick. It also leads to a lot of possibilities once you get to know it. Once you learn the basics and become familiar with your Chefman air fryer, you can feel free to experiment and modify the recipes in the way you prefer. You can prepare a wide number of dishes in the Chefman air fryer and you can adapt your favorite stove-top dish so it becomes air fryer–friendly. It all boils down to variety and lots of options, right?
Cooking perfect and delicious as well as healthy meals has never been easier. You can see how this recipe collection proves itself.

Enjoy!

Air Fryer Asparagus
PREP: 5 MINUTES • COOK TIME: 8 MINUTES
• TOTAL: 13 MINUTES
SERVES: 2

Ingredients
Nutritional yeast
Olive oil non-stick spray
One bunch of asparagus

Directions

1. **Preparing the Ingredients.** Wash asparagus and then trim off thick, woody ends.
   Spray asparagus with olive oil spray and sprinkle with yeast.
2. **Air Frying.** In your Chefman air fryer, lay asparagus in a singular layer. Set the temperature to 360°F, and set time to 8 minutes.

PER SERVING: CALORIES: 17; FAT: 4G; PROTEIN: 9G

Almond Flour Battered And Crisped Onion Rings
PREP: 5 MINUTES • COOK TIME: 15 MINUTES • TOTAL: 20 MINUTES
SERVES: 3

Ingredients
½ cup almond flour
¾ cup coconut milk
1 big white onion, sliced into rings
1 egg, beaten
1 tablespoon baking powder
1 tablespoon smoked paprika
Salt and pepper to taste

Directions
1. **Preparing the Ingredients.** Preheat the air fryer for 5 minutes.
   In a mixing bowl, mix the almond flour, baking powder, smoked paprika, salt and pepper.
   In another bowl, combine the eggs and coconut milk.
   Soak the onion slices into the egg mixture.
   Dredge the onion slices in the almond flour mixture.
2. **Air Frying.** Place in the air fryer basket.
   Close and cook for 15 minutes at 325 °F.
   Halfway through the cooking time, shake the fryer basket for even cooking.

PER SERVING: CALORIES: 217; FAT: 17.9G; PROTEIN: 5.3G

Asparagus Strata

PREP: 12 MINUTES • COOK TIME: 17 MINUTES • TOTAL: 29 MINUTES
SERVES: 4

Ingredients

6 asparagus spears, cut into 2-inch pieces
2 slices whole-wheat bread, cut into ½-inch cubes
4 eggs
3 tablespoons whole milk
½ cup grated Havarti or Swiss cheese
2 tablespoons chopped flat-leaf parsley
Pinch salt
Freshly ground black pepper

Directions

1 **Preparing the Ingredients.** Place the asparagus spears and 1 tablespoon water in a 6-inch baking pan and place in the Chefman air fryer basket. Bake for 3 to 5 minutes or until crisp and tender. Remove the asparagus from the pan and drain it. Spray the pan with nonstick cooking spray. Arrange the bread cubes and asparagus into the pan and set aside. In a medium bowl, beat the eggs with the milk until combined. Add the cheese, parsley, salt, and pepper. Pour into the baking pan. Bake for 11 to 14 minutes or until the eggs are set and the top starts to brown.

PER SERVING: CALORIES: 166; FAT: 49G; PROTEIN: 12G; FIBER: 2G

Jalapeño Poppers

PREP: 10 MINUTES • COOK TIME: 10 MINUTES • TOTAL: 20 MINUTES
SERVES: 4

Ingredients

12-18 whole fresh jalapeño
1 cup nonfat refried beans
1 cup shredded Monterey Jack or extra-sharp cheddar cheese
1 scallion, sliced
1 teaspoon salt, divided
1/4 cup all-purpose flour
2 large eggs
1/2 cup fine cornmeal
Olive oil or canola oil cooking spray

Directions

1 **Preparing the Ingredients.** Start by slicing each jalapeño lengthwise on one side. Place the jalapeños side by side in a microwave safe bowl and microwave them until they are slightly soft; usually around 5 minutes.

While your jalapeños cook; mix refried beans, scallions, 1/2 teaspoon salt, and cheese in a bowl.

Once your jalapeños are softened you can scoop out the seeds and add one tablespoon of your refried bean mixture (It can be a little less if the pepper is smaller.) Press the jalapeño closed around the filling.

Beat your eggs in a small bowl and place your flour in a separate bowl. In a third bowl mix your cornmeal and the remaining salt in a third bowl.

Roll each pepper in the flour, then dip it in the egg, and finally roll it in the cornmeal making sure to coat the entire pepper.

Place the peppers on a flat surface and coat them with a cooking spray; olive oil cooking spray is suggested.

2   **Air Frying.** Cook in your Chefman air fryer at 400 degrees for 5 minutes, turn each pepper, and then cook for another 5 minutes; serve hot.

PER SERVING: CALORIES: 244; FAT: 12G; PROTEIN: 12G; FIBER: 2.4G

Parmesan Breaded Zucchini Chips
PREP: 15 MINUTES • COOK TIME: 20 MINUTES • TOTAL: 35 MINUTES
SERVES: 5

Ingredients
For the zucchini chips:
2 medium zucchini
2 eggs
⅓ cup bread crumbs
⅓ cup grated Parmesan cheese
Salt
Pepper
Cooking oil
For the lemon aioli:
½ cup mayonnaise
½ tablespoon olive oil
Juice of ½ lemon
1 teaspoon minced garlic
Salt
Pepper

Directions
1   **Preparing the Ingredients.** To make the zucchini chips:
Slice the zucchini into thin chips (about ⅛ inch thick) using a knife or mandoline.
In a small bowl, beat the eggs. In another small bowl, combine the bread crumbs, Parmesan cheese, and salt and pepper to taste.
Spray the Chefman air fryer basket with cooking oil.
Dip the zucchini slices one at a time in the eggs and then the bread crumb mixture. You can also sprinkle the bread crumbs onto the zucchini slices with a spoon.
Place the zucchini chips in the Chefman air fryer basket, but do not stack.
2   **Air Frying.** Cook in batches. Spray the chips with cooking oil from a distance (otherwise, the breading may fly off). Cook for 10 minutes.

Remove the cooked zucchini chips from the air fryer, then repeat step 5 with the remaining zucchini.

To make the lemon aioli:
While the zucchini is cooking, combine the mayonnaise, olive oil, lemon juice, and garlic in a small bowl, adding salt and pepper to taste. Mix well until fully combined.
Cool the zucchini and serve alongside the aioli.

PER SERVING: CALORIES: 192; FAT: 13G; PROTEIN: 6G; FIBER: 4G

Bell Pepper-Corn Wrapped in Tortilla
PREP: 5 MINUTES • COOK TIME: 15 MINUTES • TOTAL: 20 MINUTES
SERVES: 4

Ingredients
1 small red bell pepper, chopped
1 small yellow onion, diced
1 tablespoon water
2 cobs grilled corn kernels
4 large tortillas
4 pieces commercial vegan nuggets, chopped
mixed greens for garnish

Directions
1. **Preparing the Ingredients.** Preheat the air fryer to 400°F.
   In a skillet heated over medium heat, water sauté the vegan nuggets together with the onions, bell peppers, and corn kernels. Set aside.
   Place filling inside the corn tortillas.
2. **Air Frying.** Fold the tortillas and place inside the air fryer and cook for 15 minutes until the tortilla wraps are crispy.
   Serve with mix greens on top.

PER SERVING: CALORIES: 548; FAT: 20.7G; PROTEIN: 46G

Baked Cheesy Eggplant with Marinara
PREP: 5 MINUTES • COOK TIME: 45 MINUTES • TOTAL: 50 MINUTES
SERVES: 3

Ingredients

1 clove garlic, sliced
1 large eggplants
1 tablespoon olive oil
1 tablespoon olive oil
1/2 pinch salt, or as needed
1/4 cup and 2 tablespoons dry bread crumbs
1/4 cup and 2 tablespoons ricotta cheese
1/4 cup grated Parmesan cheese
1/4 cup grated Parmesan cheese
1/4 cup water, plus more as needed
1/4 teaspoon red pepper flakes
1-1/2 cups prepared marinara sauce
1-1/2 teaspoons olive oil
2 tablespoons shredded pepper jack cheese
salt and freshly ground black pepper to taste

Directions
1. **Preparing the Ingredients.** Cut eggplant crosswise in 5 pieces. Peel and chop two pieces into ½-inch cubes.
   Lightly grease baking pan of air fryer with 1 tbsp olive oil for 5 minutes, heat oil at 390°F. Add half eggplant strips and cook for 2 minutes per side. Transfer to a plate.
   Add 1 ½ tsp olive oil and add garlic. Cook for a minute. Add chopped eggplants. Season with pepper flakes and salt. Cook for 4 minutes. Lower heat to 330°F. and continue cooking eggplants until soft, around 8 minutes more.
   Stir in water and marinara sauce. Cook for 7 minutes until heated through. Stirring every now and then. Transfer to a bowl.
   In a bowl, whisk well pepper, salt, pepper jack cheese, Parmesan cheese, and ricotta.
   Evenly spread cheeses over eggplant strips and then fold in half.
   Lay folded eggplant in baking pan. Pour marinara sauce on top.
   In a small bowl whisk well olive oil, and bread crumbs. Sprinkle all over sauce.
2. **Air Frying.** Cook for 15 minutes at 390°F until tops are lightly browned.
   Serve and enjoy.

PER SERVING: CALORIES: 405; FAT: 21.4G; PROTEIN: 12.7G

Spicy Sweet Potato Fries

PREP: 5 MINUTES • COOK TIME: 37 MINUTES • TOTAL: 45 MINUTES
SERVES: 4

Ingredients

2 tbsp. sweet potato fry seasoning mix
2 tbsp. olive oil
2 sweet potatoes
 Seasoning Mix:
 2 tbsp. salt
1 tbsp. cayenne pepper
1 tbsp. dried oregano
1 tbsp. fennel
2 tbsp. coriander

Directions:

1. **Preparing the Ingredients.** Slice both ends off sweet potatoes and peel. Slice lengthwise in half and again crosswise to make four pieces from each potato.
Slice each potato piece into 2-3 slices, then slice into fries.
Grind together all of seasoning mix ingredients and mix in the salt.
Ensure the Chefman air fryer is preheated to 350 degrees.
Toss potato pieces in olive oil, sprinkling with seasoning mix and tossing well to coat thoroughly.
2. **Air Frying.** Add fries to air fryer basket. Set temperature to 350°F, and set time to 27 minutes. Select START/STOP to begin. Take out the basket and turn fries. Turn off air fryer and let cook 10-12 minutes till fries are golden.

PER SERVING: CALORIES: 89; FAT: 14G; PROTEIN: 8Gs; SUGAR:3G

Creamy Spinach Quiche

PREP: 10 MINUTES • COOK TIME: 20 MINUTES • TOTAL: 30 MINUTES
SERVES: 4

Ingredients

Premade quiche crust, chilled and rolled flat to a 7-inch round
eggs
¼ cup of milk
Pinch of salt and pepper
1 clove of garlic, peeled and finely minced
½ cup of cooked spinach, drained and coarsely chopped
¼ cup of shredded mozzarella cheese
¼ cup of shredded cheddar cheese

Directions

1. **Preparing the Ingredients.** Preheat the Chefman air fryer to 360 degrees.
Press the premade crust into a 7-inch pie tin, or any appropriately sized glass or ceramic heat-safe dish. Press and trim at the edges if necessary. With a fork, pierce several holes in the dough to allow air circulation and prevent cracking of the crust while cooking.
In a mixing bowl, beat the eggs until fluffy and until the yolks and white are evenly combined.
Add milk, garlic, spinach, salt and pepper, and half the cheddar and mozzarella cheese to the eggs. Set the rest of the cheese aside for now, and stir the mixture until completely blended. Make sure the spinach is not clumped together, but rather spread among the other ingredients.
Pour the mixture into the pie crust, slowly and carefully to avoid splashing. The mixture should almost fill the crust, but not completely – leaving a ¼ inch of crust at the edges.

2. **Air Frying.** Set the air-fryer timer for 15 minutes. After15 minutes, the air fryer will shut off, and the quiche will already be firm and the crust beginning to brown. Sprinkle the rest of the cheddar and mozzarella cheese on top of the quiche filling. Reset the Chefman air fryer at 360 degrees for 5 minutes. After 5 minutes, when the Chefman air fryer shuts off, the cheese will have formed an exquisite crust on top and the quiche will be golden brown and perfect. Remove from the Chefman air fryer using oven mitts or tongs, and set on a heat-safe surface to cool for a few minutes before cutting.

Air Fryer Cauliflower Rice
PREP: 5 MINUTES • COOK TIME: 20 MINUTES • TOTAL: 25 MINUTES
SERVES: 4

Ingredients
Round 1:
 tsp. turmeric
1 C. diced carrot
½ C. diced onion
2 tbsp. low-sodium soy sauce
½ block of extra firm tofu
 Round 2:
 ½ C. frozen peas
2 minced garlic cloves
½ C. chopped broccoli
1 tbsp. minced ginger
1 tbsp. rice vinegar
1 ½ tsp. toasted sesame oil
2 tbsp. reduced-sodium soy sauce
3 C. riced cauliflower

Directions:
1 **Preparing the Ingredients.** Crumble tofu in a large bowl and toss with all the Round one ingredient.
2 **Air Frying.** Preheat the Chefman air fryer to 370 degrees, set temperature to 370°F, and set time to 10 minutes and cook 10 minutes, making sure to shake once.
In another bowl, toss ingredients from Round 2 together.
Add Round 2 mixture to air fryer and cook another 10 minutes, ensuring to shake 5 minutes in.
Enjoy!

PER SERVING: CALORIES: 67; FAT: 8G; PROTEIN: 3G; SUGAR:0G

Brown Rice, Spinach and Tofu Frittata

PREP: 5 MINUTES • COOK TIME: 55 MINUTES • TOTAL: 60 MINUTES
SERVES: 4

Ingredients

½ cup baby spinach, chopped
½ cup kale, chopped
½ onion, chopped
½ teaspoon turmeric
1 ¾ cups brown rice, cooked
1 flax egg (1 tablespoon flaxseed meal + 3 tablespoon cold water)
1 package firm tofu
1 tablespoon olive oil
1 yellow pepper, chopped
2 tablespoons soy sauce
2 teaspoons arrowroot powder
2 teaspoons Dijon mustard
2/3 cup almond milk
3 big mushrooms, chopped
3 tablespoons nutritional yeast
4 cloves garlic, crushed
4 spring onions, chopped
a handful of basil leaves, chopped

Directions:

1. **Preparing the Ingredients.** Preheat the air fryer to 375°F. Grease a pan that will fit inside the air fryer.

   Prepare the frittata crust by mixing the brown rice and flax egg. Press the rice onto the baking dish until you form a crust. Brush with a little oil and cook for 10 minutes.

   Meanwhile, heat olive oil in a skillet over medium flame and sauté the garlic and onions for 2 minutes.

   Add the pepper and mushroom and continue stirring for 3 minutes.

   Stir in the kale, spinach, spring onions, and basil. Remove from the pan and set aside.

   In a food processor, pulse together the tofu, mustard, turmeric, soy sauce, nutritional yeast, vegan milk and arrowroot powder. Pour in a mixing bowl and stir in the sautéed vegetables.

2. **Air Frying** Pour the vegan frittata mixture over the rice crust and cook in the air fryer for 40 minutes.

PER SERVING: CALORIES: 226; FAT: 8.05G; PROTEIN: 10.6G

Stuffed Mushrooms

PREP: 7 MINUTES • COOK TIME: 8 MINUTES • TOTAL: 15 MINUTES
SERVES: 12

Ingredients

2 Rashers Bacon, Diced
½ Onion, Diced
½ Bell Pepper, Diced
1 Small Carrot, Diced
24 Medium Size Mushrooms (Separate the caps & stalks)
1 cup Shredded Cheddar Plus Extra for the Top
½ cup Sour Cream

Directions:

1. **Preparing the Ingredients.** Chop the mushrooms stalks finely and fry them up with the bacon, onion, pepper and carrot at 350 ° for 8 minutes.

   When the veggies are fairly tender, stir in the sour cream & the cheese. Keep on the heat until the cheese has melted and everything is mixed nicely.

   Now grab the mushroom caps and heap a plop of filling on each one.

   Place in the fryer basket and top with a little extra cheese.

Air Fried Carrots, Yellow Squash & Zucchini

PREP: 5 MINUTES • COOK TIME: 35 MINUTES • TOTAL: 40 MINUTES
SERVES: 4

Ingredients

1 tbsp. chopped tarragon leaves
½ tsp. white pepper
1 tsp. salt
1 pound yellow squash
1 pound zucchini
6 tsp. olive oil
½ pound carrots

Directions:

1. **Preparing the Ingredients.** Stem and root the end of squash and zucchini and cut in ¾-inch half-moons. Peel and cut carrots into 1-inch cubes

   Combine carrot cubes with 2 teaspoons of olive oil, tossing to combine.

2. **Air Frying.** Pour into the Chefman air fryer basket, set temperature to 400°F, and set time to 5 minutes.

   As carrots cook, drizzle remaining olive oil over squash and zucchini pieces, then season with pepper and salt. Toss well to coat.

   Add squash and zucchini when the timer for carrots goes off. Cook 30 minutes, making sure to toss 2-3 times during the cooking process.

   Once done, take out veggies and toss with tarragon. Serve up warm!

PER SERVING: CALORIES: 122; FAT: 9G; PROTEIN: 6G; SUGAR:0G

Winter Vegetarian Frittata

PREP: 5 MINUTES • COOK TIME: 30 MINUTES • TOTAL: 35 MINUTES
SERVES: 4

Ingredients

1 leek, peeled and thinly sliced into rings
2 cloves garlic, finely minced
3 medium-sized carrots, finely chopped
2 tablespoons olive oil
6 large-sized eggs
Sea salt and ground black pepper, to taste
1/2 teaspoon dried marjoram, finely minced
1/2 cup yellow cheese of choice

Directions:

1 **Preparing the Ingredients.** Sauté the leek, garlic, and carrot in hot olive oil until they are tender and fragrant; reserve.
In the meantime, preheat your Chefman air fryer to 330 degrees F.
In a bowl, whisk the eggs along with the salt, ground black pepper, and marjoram.
Then, grease the inside of your baking dish with a nonstick cooking spray. Pour the whisked eggs into the baking dish. Stir in the sautéed carrot mixture. Top with the cheese shreds.
2 **Air Frying.** Place the baking dish in the Chefman air fryer cooking basket. Cook about 30 minutes and serve warm.

Brussels Sprouts with Balsamic Oil

PREP: 5 MINUTES • COOK TIME: 15 MINUTES • TOTAL: 20 MINUTES
SERVES: 4

Ingredients

¼ teaspoon salt
1 tablespoon balsamic vinegar
2 cups Brussels sprouts, halved
3 tablespoons olive oil

Directions:

1 **Preparing the Ingredients.** Preheat the air fryer for 5 minutes.
Mix all ingredients in a bowl until the zucchini fries are well coated.
2 **Air Frying.** Place in the air fryer basket. Close and cook for 15 minutes for 350°F.

PER SERVING: CALORIES: 82; FAT: 6.8G; PROTEIN: 1.5G

Air Fried Kale Chips

PREP: 5 MINUTES • COOK TIME: 10 MINUTES • TOTAL: 15 MINUTES
SERVES: 6

Ingredients

¼ tsp. Himalayan salt
3 tbsp. yeast
Avocado oil
1 bunch of kale

Directions:

1. **Preparing the Ingredients.** Rinse kale and with paper towels, dry well.
   Tear kale leaves into large pieces.
   Remember they will shrink as they cook so good sized pieces are necessary.
   Place kale pieces in a bowl and spritz with avocado oil till shiny. Sprinkle with salt and yeast.
   With your hands, toss kale leaves well to combine.
2. **Air Frying.** Pour half of the kale mixture into the Chefman air fryer, set temperature to 350°F, and set time to 5 minutes. Remove and repeat with another half of kale.

PER SERVING: CALORIES: 55; FAT: 10G; PROTEIN: 1G; SUGAR:0G

Zucchini Omelet

PREP: 10 MINUTES • COOK TIME: 10 MINUTES • TOTAL: 20 MINUTES
SERVES: 2

Ingredients

1 teaspoon butter
1 zucchini, julienned
4 eggs
¼ teaspoon fresh basil, chopped
¼ teaspoon red pepper flakes, crushed
Salt and freshly ground black pepper, to taste

Directions:

1. **Preparing the Ingredients.** Preheat the Chefman air fryer to 355 degrees F.
   In a skillet, melt butter on medium heat.
   Add zucchini and cook for about 3-4 minutes.
   In a bowl, add the eggs, basil, red pepper flakes, salt and black pepper and beat well.
   Add cooked zucchini and gently, stir to combine.
2. **Air Frying.** Transfer the mixture into the Chefman air fryer pan.
   Cook for about 10 minutes or till done completely.

Cheesy Cauliflower Fritters

PREP: 10 MINUTES • COOK TIME: 7 MINUTES • TOTAL: 17 MINUTES
SERVES: 8

Ingredients

½ C. chopped parsley
1 C. Italian breadcrumbs
1/3 C. shredded mozzarella cheese
1/3 C. shredded sharp cheddar cheese
1 egg
2 minced garlic cloves
3 chopped scallions
1 head of cauliflower

Directions:

1 **Preparing the Ingredients.** Cut cauliflower up into florets. Wash well and pat dry. Place into a food processor and pulse 20-30 seconds till it looks like rice. Place cauliflower rice in a bowl and mix with pepper, salt, egg, cheeses, breadcrumbs, garlic, and scallions. With hands, form 15 patties of the mixture. Add more breadcrumbs if needed.
2 **Air Frying.** With olive oil, spritz patties, and place into your Chefman air fryer in a single layer. Set temperature to 390°F, and set time to 7 minutes, flipping after 7 minutes.

PER SERVING: CALORIES: 209; FAT: 17G; PROTEIN: 6G; SUGAR:0.5

Cauliflower Bites

PREP: 10 MINUTES • COOK TIME: 18 MINUTES • TOTAL: 28 MINUTES
SERVES: 4

Ingredients

1 Head Cauliflower, cut into small florets
Tsps Garlic Powder
Pinch of Salt and Pepper
1 Tbsp Butter, melted
1/2 Cup Chili Sauce
Olive Oil

Directions:

1 **Preparing the Ingredients.** Place cauliflower into a bowl and pour oil over florets to lightly cover.
Season florets with salt, pepper and the garlic powder and toss well.
2 **Air Frying.** Place florets into the Chefman air fryer at 350 degrees for 14 minutes. Remove cauliflower from the Air Fryer. Combine the melted butter with the chili sauce
Pour over the florets so that they are well coated.
Return to the Chefman air fryer and cook for additional 3 to 4 minutes
Serve as a side or with ranch or cheese dip as a snack

Buttered Carrot-Zucchini with Mayo

PREP: 10 MINUTES • COOK TIME: 25 MINUTES • TOTAL: 35 MINUTES
SERVES: 4

Ingredients

1 tablespoon grated onion
2 tablespoons butter, melted
1/2-pound carrots, sliced
1-1/2 zucchinis, sliced
1/4 cup water
1/4 cup mayonnaise
1/4 teaspoon prepared horseradish
1/4 teaspoon salt
1/4 teaspoon ground black pepper
1/4 cup Italian bread crumbs

Directions:

1 **Preparing the Ingredients.** Lightly grease baking pan of air fryer with cooking spray. Add carrots. For 8 minutes, cook on 360°F. Add zucchini and continue cooking for another 5 minutes.
Meanwhile, in a bowl whisk well pepper, salt, horseradish, onion, mayonnaise, and water. Pour into pan of veggies. Toss well to coat.
In a small bowl mix melted butter and bread crumbs. Sprinkle over veggies.
2 **Air Frying.** Cook for 10 minutes at 390°F, until tops are lightly browned.
Serve and enjoy.

PER SERVING: CALORIES: 223; FAT: 17G; PROTEIN: 2.7G; SUGAR:0.5

Avocado Fries

PREP: 10 MINUTES • COOK TIME: 7 MINUTES • TOTAL: 17 MINUTES
SERVES: 6

Ingredients

1 avocado
½ tsp. salt
½ C. panko breadcrumbs
Bean liquid (aquafaba) from a 15-ounce can of white or garbanzo beans

Directions:

1 **Preparing the Ingredients.** Peel, pit, and slice up avocado.
Toss salt and breadcrumbs together in a bowl. Place aquafaba into another bowl. Dredge slices of avocado first in aquafaba and then in panko, making sure you get an even coating.
2 **Air Frying.** Place coated avocado slices into a single layer in the Chefman air fryer. Set temperature to 390°F, and set time to 5 minutes.
Serve with your favorite keto dipping sauce!

PER SERVING: CALORIES: 102; FAT: 22G; PROTEIN:9G; SUGAR:1G

Roasted Vegetables Salad

PREP: 5 MINUTES • COOK TIME: 85 MINUTES • TOTAL: 90 MINUTES
SERVES: 5

Ingredients

3 eggplants
1 tbsp of olive oil
3 medium zucchini
1 tbsp of olive oil
4 large tomatoes, cut them in eighths
4 cups of one shaped pasta
2 peppers of any color
1 cup of sliced tomatoes cut into small cubes
2 teaspoon of salt substitute
8 tbsp of grated parmesan cheese
½ cup of Italian dressing
Leaves of fresh basil

Directions:

1 **Preparing the Ingredients.** Wash your eggplant and slice it off then discard the green end. Make sure not to peel.
Slice your eggplant into1/2 inch of thick rounds. 1/2 inch)
Pour 1tbsp of olive oil on the eggplant round.

2 **Air Frying.** Put the eggplants in the basket of the Chefman air fryer and then toss it in the air fryer. Cook the eggplants for 40 minutes. Set the heat to 360 ° F
Meanwhile, wash your zucchini and slice it then discard the green end. But do not peel it.
Slice the Zucchini into thick rounds of ½ inch each.
In the basket of the Air Fryer, toss your ingredients
Add 1 tbsp of olive oil.

3 **Air Frying.** Cook the zucchini for 25 minutes on a heat of 360° F and when the time is off set it aside.

Wash and cut the tomatoes.

4 **Air Frying.** Arrange your tomatoes in the basket of the Chefman air fryer. Set the timer to 30 minutes. Set the heat to 350° F When the time is off, cook your pasta according to the pasta guiding directions, empty it into a colander. Run the cold water on it and wash it and drain the pasta and put it aside.
Meanwhile, wash and chop your peppers and place it in a bow
Wash and thinly slice your cherry tomatoes and add it to the bowl. Add your roasted veggies.
Add the pasta, a pinch of salt, the topping dressing, add the basil and the parm and toss everything together. (It is better to mix with your hands). Set the ingredients together in the refrigerator, and let it chill
Serve your salad and enjoy it!

Cheddar, Squash 'n Zucchini Casserole

PREP: 5 MINUTES • COOK TIME: 30 MINUTES • TOTAL: 35 MINUTES

SERVES: 4

Ingredients

1 egg
5 saltine crackers, or as needed, crushed
2 tablespoons bread crumbs
1/2-pound yellow squash, sliced
1/2-pound zucchini, sliced
1/2 cup shredded Cheddar cheese
1-1/2 teaspoons white sugar
1/2 teaspoon salt
1/4 onion, diced
1/4 cup biscuit baking mix
1/4 cup butter

Directions:

1   **Preparing the Ingredients.** Lightly grease baking pan of air fryer with cooking spray. Add onion, zucchini, and yellow squash. Cover pan with foil and for 15 minutes, cook on 360° F or until tender.
Stir in salt, sugar, egg, butter, baking mix, and cheddar cheese. Mix well. Fold in crushed crackers. Top with bread crumbs.

2   **Air Frying** Cook for 15 minutes at 390° F until tops are lightly browned.
Serve and enjoy.

PER SERVING: CALORIES: 285; FAT: 20.5G; PROTEIN:8.6G

Zucchini Parmesan Chips

PREP: 10 MINUTES • COOK TIME: 8 MINUTES • TOTAL: 18 MINUTES

SERVES: 10

Ingredients

½ tsp. paprika
½ C. grated parmesan cheese
½ C. Italian breadcrumbs
1 lightly beaten egg
2 thinly sliced zucchinis

Directions:

1   **Preparing the Ingredients.** Use a very sharp knife or mandolin slicer to slice zucchini as thinly as you can. Pat off extra moisture.
Beat egg with a pinch of pepper and salt and a bit of water.
Combine paprika, cheese, and breadcrumbs in a bowl.
Dip slices of zucchini into the egg mixture and then into breadcrumb mixture. Press gently to coat.

2   **Air Frying.** With olive oil cooking spray, mist coated zucchini slices. Place into your Chefman air fryer in a single layer. Set temperature to 350°F, and set time to 8 minutes.
Sprinkle with salt and serve with salsa.

PER SERVING: CALORIES: 211; FAT: 16G; PROTEIN:8G; SUGAR:0G

Jalapeño Cheese Balls

PREP: 10 MINUTES • COOK TIME: 8 MINUTES • TOTAL: 18 MINUTES
SERVES: 12

Ingredients

4 ounces cream cheese
⅓ cup shredded mozzarella cheese
⅓ cup shredded Cheddar cheese
2 jalapeños, finely chopped
½ cup bread crumbs
2 eggs
½ cup all-purpose flour
Salt
Pepper
Cooking oil

Directions:

1 **Preparing the Ingredients.** In a medium bowl, combine the cream cheese, mozzarella, Cheddar, and jalapeños. Mix well.
   Form the cheese mixture into balls about an inch thick. Using a small ice cream scoop works well.
   Arrange the cheese balls on a sheet pan and place in the freezer for 15 minutes. This will help the cheese balls maintain their shape while frying.
   Spray the Chefman air fryer basket with cooking oil. Place the bread crumbs in a small bowl. In another small bowl, beat the eggs. In a third small bowl, combine the flour with salt and pepper to taste, and mix well. Remove the cheese balls from the freezer. Dip the cheese balls in the flour, then the eggs, and then the bread crumbs.

2 **Air Frying.** Place the cheese balls in the Chefman air fryer. Spray with cooking oil. Cook for 8 minutes.
   Open the air fryer and flip the cheese balls. I recommend flipping them instead of shaking so the balls maintain their form.

Cook an additional 4 minutes. Cool before serving.

PER SERVING: CALORIES: 96; FAT: 6G; PROTEIN:4G; SUGAR:0G

Crispy Roasted Broccoli

PREP: 10 MINUTES • COOK TIME: 8 MINUTES • TOTAL: 18 MINUTES
SERVES: 2

Ingredients

¼ tsp. Masala
½ tsp. red chili powder
½ tsp. salt
¼ tsp. turmeric powder
1 tbsp. chickpea flour
2 tbsp. yogurt
1 pound broccoli

Directions:

1 **Preparing the Ingredients.** Cut broccoli up into florets. Soak in a bowl of water with 2 teaspoons of salt for at least half an hour to remove impurities.
Take out broccoli florets from water and let drain. Wipe down thoroughly.
Mix all other ingredients together to create a marinade.
Toss broccoli florets in the marinade.
Cover and chill 15-30 minutes.
2 **Air Frying**. Preheat the Chefman air fryer to 390 degrees. Place marinated broccoli florets into the fryer, set temperature to 350°F, and set time to 10 minutes. Florets will be crispy when done.

PER SERVING: CALORIES: 96; FAT: 1.3G; PROTEIN:7G; SUGAR:4.5G

Creamy And Cheese Broccoli Bake

PREP: 5 MINUTES • COOK TIME: 30 MINUTES • TOTAL: 35 MINUTES
SERVES: 2

Ingredients

1-pound fresh broccoli, coarsely chopped
2 tablespoons all-purpose flour
salt to taste
1 tablespoon dry bread crumbs, or to taste
1/2 large onion, coarsely chopped
1/2 (14 ounce) can evaporated milk, divided
1/2 cup cubed sharp Cheddar cheese
1-1/2 teaspoons butter, or to taste
1/4 cup water

Directions:

1 **Preparing the Ingredients.** Lightly grease baking pan of air fryer with cooking spray. Mix in half of the milk and flour in pan and for 5 minutes, cook on 360°F. Halfway through cooking time, mix well. Add broccoli and remaining milk. Mix well and cook for another 5 minutes.
Stir in cheese and mix well until melted.
In a small bowl mix well, butter and bread crumbs. Sprinkle on top of broccoli.
2 **Air Frying**. Cook for 20 minutes at 360°F until tops are lightly browned.
Serve and enjoy.

PER SERVING: CALORIES: 444; FAT: 22.3G; PROTEIN:23G

Coconut Battered Cauliflower Bites

PREP: 5 MINUTES • COOK TIME: 20 MINUTES • TOTAL: 25 MINUTES
SERVES: 4

Ingredients

salt and pepper to taste
1 flax egg (1 tablespoon flaxseed meal + 3 tablespoon water)
1 small cauliflower, cut into florets
1 teaspoon mixed spice
½ teaspoon mustard powder
2 tablespoons maple syrup
1 clove of garlic, minced
2 tablespoons soy sauce
1/3 cup oats flour
1/3 cup plain flour
1/3 cup desiccated coconut

Directions:

1 **Preparing the Ingredients.** Preheat the air fryer to 400°F.

   In a mixing bowl, mix together oats, flour, and desiccated coconut. Season with salt and pepper to taste. Set aside.

   In another bowl, place the flax egg and add a pinch of salt to taste. Set aside. Season the cauliflower with mixed spice and mustard powder.

   Dredge the florets in the flax egg first then in the flour mixture.

2 **Air Frying**. Place inside the air fryer and cook for 15 minutes.

   Meanwhile, place the maple syrup, garlic, and soy sauce in a sauce pan and heat over medium flame. Bring to a boil and adjust the heat to low until the sauce thickens. After 15 minutes, take out the florets from the air fryer and place them in the saucepan.

   Toss to coat the florets and place inside the air fryer and cook for another 5 minutes.

PER SERVING: CALORIES: 154; FAT: 2.3G; PROTEIN:4.69G

Crispy Jalapeno Coins

PREP: 10 MINUTES • COOK TIME: 5 MINUTES • TOTAL: 15 MINUTES
SERVES: 2

Ingredients

1 egg
2-3 tbsp. coconut flour
1 sliced and seeded jalapeno
Pinch of garlic powder
Pinch of onion powder
Pinch of Cajun seasoning (optional)
Pinch of pepper and salt

Directions:

1 **Preparing the Ingredients.** Ensure your air fryer is preheated to 400 degrees.
Mix together all dry ingredients.
Pat jalapeno slices dry. Dip coins into egg wash and then into dry mixture. Toss to thoroughly coat.
Add coated jalapeno slices to air fryer in a singular layer. Spray with olive oil.
2 **Air Frying**. Set temperature to 350°F, and set time to 5 minutes. Cook just till crispy.

PER SERVING: CALORIES: 128; FAT: 8G; PROTEIN:7G; SUGAR:0G

Vegetable Egg Rolls

PREP: 15 MINUTES • COOK TIME: 10 MINUTES • TOTAL: 25 MINUTES
SERVES: 8

Ingredients

½ cup chopped mushrooms
½ cup grated carrots
½ cup chopped zucchini
2 green onions, chopped
2 tablespoons low-sodium soy sauce
8 egg roll wrappers
1 tablespoon cornstarch
1 egg, beaten

Directions:

1 **Preparing the Ingredients.** In a medium bowl, combine the mushrooms, carrots, zucchini, green onions, and soy sauce, and stir together. Place the egg roll wrappers on a work surface. Top each with about 3 tablespoons of the vegetable mixture.
In a small bowl, combine the cornstarch and egg and mix well. Brush some of this mixture on the edges of the egg roll wrappers. Roll up the wrappers, enclosing the vegetable filling. Brush some of the egg mixture on the outside of the egg rolls to seal.
2 **Air Frying.** Air-fry for 7 to 10 minutes or until the egg rolls are brown and crunchy.

PER SERVING: CALORIES: 112; FAT: 1G; PROTEIN:4G; FIBER:1G

Buffalo Cauliflower

PREP: 5 MINUTES • COOK TIME: 15 MINUTES • TOTAL: 20 MINUTES
SERVES: 2

Ingredients
Cauliflower:
1 C. panko breadcrumbs
1 tsp. salt
4 C. cauliflower florets
Buffalo Coating:
¼ C. Vegan Buffalo sauce
¼ C. melted vegan butter

Directions:
1 **Preparing the Ingredients.** Melt butter in microwave and whisk in buffalo sauce. Dip each cauliflower floret into buffalo mixture, ensuring it gets coated well. Hold over a bowl till floret is done dripping. Mix breadcrumbs with salt.
2 **Air Frying.** Dredge dipped florets into breadcrumbs and place into air fryer. Set temperature to 350°F, and set time to 15 minutes. When slightly browned, they are ready to eat!
Serve with your favorite keto dipping sauce!

PER SERVING: CALORIES: 194; FAT: 17G; PROTEIN:10G; SUGAR:3

Veggies on Toast

PREP: 12 MINUTES • COOK TIME: 11 MINUTES • TOTAL: 23 MINUTES
SERVES: 4

Ingredients

1 red bell pepper, cut into ½-inch strips
1 cup sliced button or cremini mushrooms
1 small yellow squash, sliced
2 green onions, cut into ½-inch slices
Extra light olive oil for misting
4 to 6 pieces sliced French or Italian bread
2 tablespoons softened butter
½ cup soft goat cheese

Directions:
1 **Preparing the Ingredients.** Combine the red pepper, mushrooms, squash, and green onions in the Chefman air fryer and mist with oil.
2 **Air Frying.** Roast for 7 to 9 minutes or until the vegetables are tender, shaking the basket once during cooking time.
Remove the vegetables from the basket and set aside. Spread the bread with butter and place in the Chefman air fryer, butter-side up.
3 **Air Frying.** Toast for 2 to 4 minutes or until golden brown. Spread the goat cheese on the toasted bread and top with the vegetables; serve warm.

PER SERVING: CALORIES: 162; FAT: 11G; PROTEIN:7G; FIBER:2G

Crisped Baked Cheese Stuffed Chile Pepper

PREP: 10 MINUTES • COOK TIME: 30 MINUTES • TOTAL: 40 MINUTES
SERVES: 3

Ingredients
1 (7 ounce) can whole green Chile peppers, drained
1 egg, beaten
1 tablespoon all-purpose flour
1/2 (5 ounce) can evaporated milk
1/2 (8 ounce) can tomato sauce
1/4-pound Monterey Jack cheese, shredded
1/4-pound Longhorn or Cheddar cheese, shredded
1/4 cup milk

Directions:
1 **Preparing the Ingredients.** Lightly grease baking pan of air fryer with cooking spray. Evenly spread chilies and sprinkle cheddar and Jack cheese on top.
In a bowl whisk well flour, milk, and eggs. Pour over chilies.
2 **Air Frying.** For 20 minutes, cook on 360°F Add tomato sauce on top.
Cook for 10 minutes at 390°F until tops are lightly browned.
Serve and enjoy.

PER SERVING: CALORIES: 392; FAT: 27.6G; PROTEIN:23.9G

Jicama Fries

PREP: 10 MINUTES • COOK TIME: 5 MINUTES • TOTAL: 15 MINUTES
SERVES: 8

Ingredients
1 tbsp. dried thyme
¾ C. arrowroot flour
½ large Jicama
eggs

Directions:
1 **Preparing the Ingredients.** Sliced jicama into fries.
Whisk eggs together and pour over fries. Toss to coat.
Mix a pinch of salt, thyme, and arrowroot flour together. Toss egg-coated jicama into dry mixture, tossing to coat well.
2 **Air Frying.** Spray the Chefman air fryer basket with olive oil and add fries. Set temperature to 350°F, and set time to 5 minutes. Toss halfway into the cooking process.

PER SERVING: CALORIES: 211; FAT: 19G; PROTEIN:9G; SUGAR:1

Jumbo Stuffed Mushrooms

PREP: 10 MINUTES • COOK TIME: 20 MINUTES • TOTAL: 30 MINUTES
SERVES: 4

Ingredients

4 jumbo portobello mushrooms
1 tablespoon olive oil
¼ cup ricotta cheese
5 tablespoons Parmesan cheese, divided
1 cup frozen chopped spinach, thawed and drained
⅓ cup bread crumbs
¼ teaspoon minced fresh rosemary

Directions:

1 **Preparing the Ingredients.** Wipe the mushrooms with a damp cloth. Remove the stems and discard. Using a spoon, gently scrape out most of the gills.
Rub the mushrooms with the olive oil.
2 **Air Frying** Put in the Chefman air fryer basket, hollow side up, and bake for 3 minutes. Carefully remove the mushroom caps, because they will contain liquid. Drain the liquid out of the caps.
In a medium bowl, combine the ricotta, 3 tablespoons of Parmesan cheese, spinach, bread crumbs, and rosemary, and mix well. Stuff this mixture into the drained mushroom caps. Sprinkle with the remaining 2 tablespoons of Parmesan cheese.
Put the mushroom caps back into the basket and bake for 4 to 6 minutes or until the filling is hot and the mushroom caps are tender.

PER SERVING: CALORIES: 117; FAT: 7G; PROTEIN:7G; FIBER:1G

Air Fryer Brussels Sprouts

PREP: 10 MINUTES • COOK TIME: 10 MINUTES • TOTAL: 20 MINUTES
SERVES: 8

Ingredients

¼ tsp. salt
1 tbsp. balsamic vinegar
1 tbsp. olive oil
2 C. Brussels sprouts

Directions:

1 **Preparing the Ingredients.** Cut Brussels sprouts in half lengthwise. Toss with salt, vinegar, and olive oil till coated thoroughly.
2 **Air Frying.** Add coated sprouts to the Chefman air fryer, close crisping lid, set temperature to 400°F, and set time to 10 minutes. Shake after 5 minutes of cooking. Brussels sprouts are ready to devour when brown and crisp!

PER SERVING: CALORIES: 118; FAT: 9G; PROTEIN:11G; SUGAR:1

Spaghetti Squash Tots

PREP: 10 MINUTES • COOK TIME: 15 MINUTES • TOTAL: 25 MINUTES
SERVES: 8

Ingredients

¼ tsp. pepper
½ tsp. salt
1 thinly sliced scallion
1 spaghetti squash

Directions:

1   **Preparing the Ingredients.** Wash and cut the squash in half lengthwise. Scrape out the seeds.
    With a fork, remove spaghetti meat by strands and throw out skins.
    In a clean towel, toss in squash and wring out as much moisture as possible. Place in a bowl and with a knife slice through meat a few times to cut up smaller.
    Add pepper, salt, and scallions to squash and mix well.
2   **Air Frying.** Create "tot" shapes with your hands and place in the Chefman air fryer. Spray with olive oil. Set temperature to 350°F, and set time to 15 minutes. Cook until golden and crispy!

PER SERVING: CALORIES: 231; FAT: 18G; PROTEIN:5G; SUGAR:0G

Crispy And Healthy Avocado Fingers

PREP: 10 MINUTES • COOK TIME: 10 MINUTES • TOTAL: 20 MINUTES
SERVES: 4

Ingredients

½ cup panko breadcrumbs
½ teaspoon salt
1 pitted Haas avocado, peeled and sliced
liquid from 1 can white beans or aquafaba

Directions:

1   **Preparing the Ingredients.** Preheat the air fryer at 350°F.
    In a shallow bowl, toss the breadcrumbs and salt until well combined.
    Dredge the avocado slices first with the aquafaba then in the breadcrumb mixture. Place the avocado slices in a single layer inside the air fryer basket.
2   **Air Frying.** Cook for 10 minutes and shake halfway through the cooking time.

PER SERVING: CALORIES: 51; FAT: 7.5G; PROTEIN:1.39G

Onion Rings

PREP: 10 MINUTES • COOK TIME: 10 MINUTES • TOTAL: 20 MINUTES
SERVES: 4

Ingredients

1 large spanish onion
1/2 cup buttermilk
2 eggs, lightly beaten
3/4 cups unbleached all-purpose flour
3/4 cups panko bread crumbs
1/2 teaspoon baking powder
1/2 teaspoon Cayenne pepper, to taste
Salt

Directions:

1 **Preparing the Ingredients.** Start by cutting your onion into 1/2 thick rings and separate. Smaller pieces can be discarded or saved for other recipes.
Beat the eggs in a large bowl and mix in the buttermilk, then set it aside.
In another bowl combine flour, pepper, bread crumbs, and baking powder.
Use a large spoon to dip a whole ring in the buttermilk, then pull it through the flour mix on both sides to completely coat the ring.

2 **Air Frying.** Cook about 8 rings at a time in your Chefman air fryer for 8-10 minutes at 360 degrees shaking half way through.

PER SERVING: CALORIES: 225; FAT: 3.8G; PROTEIN:19G; FIBER:2.4G

Cinnamon Butternut Squash Fries

PREP: 5 MINUTES • COOK TIME: 10 MINUTES • TOTAL: 15 MINUTES
SERVES: 8

Ingredients

1 pinch of salt
1 tbsp. powdered unprocessed sugar
½ tsp. nutmeg
2 tsp. cinnamon
1 tbsp. coconut oil
10 ounces pre-cut butternut squash fries

Directions:

1 **Preparing the Ingredients.** In a plastic bag, pour in all ingredients. Coat fries with other components till coated and sugar is dissolved.

2 **Air Frying.** Spread coated fries into a single layer in the Chefman air fryer. Set temperature to 390°F, and set time to 10 minutes. Cook until crispy.

PER SERVING: CALORIES: 175; FAT: 8G; PROTEIN:1G; SUGAR

Korean Chicken Wings

PREP: 5 MINUTES • COOK TIME: 10 MINUTES • TOTAL: 15 MINUTES SERVES: 8

Ingredients
Wings:
1 tsp. pepper
1 tsp. salt
2 pounds chicken wings
Sauce:
2 packets Splenda
1 tbsp. minced garlic
1 tbsp. minced ginger
1 tbsp. sesame oil
1 tsp. agave nectar
1 tbsp. mayo
2 tbsp. gochujang
 Finishing:
¼ C. chopped green onions
2 tsp. sesame seeds

Directions:
1 **Preparing the Ingredients.** Ensure air fryer is preheated to 400 degrees.
   Line a small pan with foil and place a rack onto the pan, then place into air fryer.
   Season wings with pepper and salt and place onto the rack.
2 **Air Frying.** Set temperature to 160°F, and set time to 20 minutes and air fry 20 minutes, turning at 10 minutes.
   As chicken air fries, mix together all the sauce components.
   Once a thermometer says that the chicken has reached 160 degrees, take out wings and place into a bowl.
   Pour half of the sauce mixture over wings, tossing well to coat.

Put coated wings back into air fryer for 5 minutes or till they reach 165 degrees. Remove and sprinkle with green onions and sesame seeds. Dip into extra sauce.

PER SERVING: CALORIES: 356; FAT: 26G; PROTEIN:23G; SUGAR:2G

Almond Flour Coco-Milk Battered Chicken

PREP: 5 MINUTES • COOK TIME: 30 MINUTES • TOTAL: 35 MINUTES
SERVES: 4

Ingredients
¼ cup coconut milk
½ cup almond flour
1 ½ tablespoons old bay Cajun seasoning
1 egg, beaten
4 small chicken thighs
Salt and pepper to taste

Directions:
1 **Preparing the Ingredients.** Preheat the air fryer for 5 minutes.
Mix the egg and coconut milk in a bowl.
Soak the chicken thighs in the beaten egg mixture.
In a mixing bowl, combine the almond flour, Cajun seasoning, salt and pepper.
Dredge the chicken thighs in the almond flour mixture.
Place in the air fryer basket.
2 **Air Frying** Cook for 30 minutes at 350°F.

PER SERVING: CALORIES: 590; FAT: 38G; PROTEIN:32.5G; CARBS:3.2G

Sweet And Sour Chicken

PREP: 5 MINUTES • COOK TIME: 20 MINUTES • TOTAL: 25 MINUTES
SERVES: 6

Ingredients
3 Chicken Breasts, cubed
1/2 Cup Flour
1/2 Cup Cornstarch
2 Red Peppers, sliced
1Onion,chopped
2 Carrots, julienned
3/4 Cup Sugar
2 Tbsps Cornstarch
1/3 Cup Vinegar
2/3 Cup Water
1/4 cup Soy sauce
1 Tbsp Ketchup

Directions:
1. **Preparing the Ingredients.** Preheat the Chefman air fryer to 375 degrees.
Combine the flour, cornstarch and chicken in an air tight container and shake to combine
Remove chicken from the container and shake off any excess flour.
2. **Air Frying.** Add chicken to the Air Fryer tray and cook for 20 minutes.
In a saucepan, whisk together sugar, water, vinegar, soy sauce and ketchup.
Bring to a boil over medium heat, reduce the heat then simmer for 2 minutes
After cooking the chicken for 20 minutes, add the vegetables and sauce mixture to the Chefman air fryer and cook for another 5 minutes
Serve over hot rice

Perfect Chicken Parmesan

PREP: 5 MINUTES • COOK TIME: 25 MINUTES • TOTAL: 30 MINUTES
SERVES: 2

Ingredients

2 large white meat chicken breasts, approximately 5-6 ounces
1 cup of breadcrumbs (Panko brand works well)
2 medium-sized eggs
Pinch of salt and pepper
1 tablespoon of dried oregano
1 cup of marinara sauce (store-bought or homemade will do equally well)
2 slices of provolone cheese
1 tablespoon of parmesan cheese

Directions:

1. **Preparing the Ingredients.** Cover the basket of the Chefman air fryer with a lining of tin foil, leaving the edges uncovered to allow air to circulate through the basket.

   Preheat the air fryer to 350 degrees.

   In a mixing bowl, beat the eggs until fluffy and until the yolks and whites are fully combined, and set aside.

   In a separate mixing bowl, combine the breadcrumbs, oregano, salt and pepper, and set aside.

   One by one, dip the raw chicken breasts into the bowl with dry ingredients, coating both sides; then submerge into the bowl with wet ingredients, then dip again into the dry ingredients. This double coating will ensure an extra crisp-and-delicious air-fry!

   Lay the coated chicken breasts on the foil covering the Chefman air fryer basket, in a single flat layer.

2. **Air Frying.** Set the Chefman air fryer timer for 10 minutes.

   After 10 minutes, the air fryer will turn off and the chicken should be mid-way cooked and the breaded coating starting to brown.

   Using tongs, turn each piece of chicken over to ensure a full all-over fry.

   Reset the air fryer to 320 degrees for another 10 minutes.

   While the chicken is cooking, pour half the marinara sauce into a 7-inch heat-safe pan.

   After 15 minutes, when the air fryer shuts off, remove the fried chicken breasts using tongs and set in the marinara-covered pan. Drizzle the rest of the marinara sauce over the fried chicken, then place the slices of provolone cheese atop both of them and sprinkle the parmesan cheese over the entire pan.

   Reset the air fryer to 350 degrees for 5 minutes.

   After 5 minutes, when the air fryer shuts off, remove the dish from the air fryer using tongs or oven mitts. The chicken will be perfectly crisped and the cheese melted and lightly toasted. Serve while hot!

Basil-Garlic Breaded Chicken Bake
PREP: 5 MINUTES • COOK TIME: 25 MINUTES • TOTAL: 30 MINUTES
SERVES: 2

Ingredients
2 boneless skinless chicken breast halves (4 ounces each)
1 tablespoon butter, melted
1 large tomato, seeded and chopped
2 garlic cloves, minced
1 1/2 tablespoons minced fresh basil
1/2 tablespoon olive oil
1/2 teaspoon salt
1/4 cup all-purpose flour
1/4 cup egg substitute
1/4 cup grated Parmesan cheese
1/4 cup dry bread crumbs
1/4 teaspoon pepper

Directions:
1 **Preparing the Ingredients.** In shallow bowl, whisk well egg substitute and place flour in a separate bowl. Dip chicken in flour, then egg, and then flour. In small bowl whisk well butter, bread crumbs and cheese. Sprinkle over chicken.
Lightly grease baking pan of air fryer with cooking spray. Place breaded chicken on bottom of pan. Cover with foil.
2 **Air Frying.** For 20 minutes, cook on 390°F.
Meanwhile, in a bowl whisk well remaining ingredient.
Remove foil from pan and then pour over chicken the remaining Ingredients.
Cook for 8 minutes.
Serve and enjoy.

PER SERVING: CALORIES: 311; FAT: 11G; PROTEIN:31G; CARBS:22G

Buffalo Chicken Wings
PREP: 5 MINUTES • COOK TIME: 30 MINUTES • TOTAL: 35 MINUTES
SERVES: 8

Ingredients
1 tsp. salt
1-2 tbsp. brown sugar
1 tbsp. Worcestershire sauce
½ C. vegan butter
½ C. cayenne pepper sauce
4 pounds chicken wings

Directions:
1 **Preparing the Ingredients.** Whisk salt, brown sugar, Worcestershire sauce, butter, and hot sauce together and set to the side.
Dry wings and add to air fryer basket.
2 **Air Frying.** Set temperature to 380°F, and set time to 25 minutes. Cook tossing halfway through.
When timer sounds, shake wings and bump up the temperature to 400 degrees and cook another 5 minutes.
Take out wings and place into a big bowl.
Add sauce and toss well.
Serve alongside celery sticks!

PER SERVING: CALORIES: 402; FAT: 16G; PROTEIN:17G; SUGAR:4G

Zingy & Nutty Chicken Wings

PREP: 5 MINUTES • COOK TIME: 18 MINUTES • TOTAL: 23 MINUTES
SERVES: 4

Ingredients

1 tablespoon fish sauce
1 tablespoon fresh lemon juice
1 teaspoon sugar
12 chicken middle wings, cut into half
2 fresh lemongrass stalks, chopped finely
¼ cup unsalted cashews, crushed

Directions:

1. **Preparing the Ingredients.** In a bowl, mix together fish sauce, lime juice and sugar. Add wings ad coat with mixture generously. Refrigerate to marinate for about 1-2 hours.
Preheat the air fryer to 355 degrees F.
2. **Air Frying.** In the Chefman air fryer pan, place lemongrass stalks. Cook for about 2-3 minutes. Remove the cashew mixture from Air fryer and transfer into a bowl. Now, set the Chefman air fryer to 390 degrees F.
Place the chicken wings in Air fryer pan. Cook for about 13-15 minutes further.
Transfer the wings into serving plates. Sprinkle with cashew mixture and serve.

Honey and Wine Chicken Breasts

PREP: 5 MINUTES • COOK TIME: 15 MINUTES • TOTAL: 20 MINUTES
SERVES: 4

Ingredients

2 chicken breasts, rinsed and halved
1 tablespoon melted butter
1/2 teaspoon freshly ground pepper, or to taste
3/4 teaspoon sea salt, or to taste
1 teaspoon paprika
1 teaspoon dried rosemary
2 tablespoons dry white wine
1 tablespoon honey

Directions:

1. **Preparing the Ingredients.** Firstly, pat the chicken breasts dry. Lightly coat them with the melted butter.
Then, add the remaining ingredients.
2. **Air Frying.** Transfer them to the air fryer basket; bake about 15 minutes at 330 degrees F. Serve warm and enjoy!
3.

PER SERVING: CALORIES: 189; FAT: 14G; PROTEIN:11G; SUGAR:1G

Chicken Fillets, Brie & Ham

PREP: 5 MINUTES • COOK TIME: 15 MINUTES • TOTAL: 20 MINUTES
SERVES: 4

Ingredients

2 Large Chicken Fillets
Freshly Ground Black Pepper
4 Small Slices of Brie (Or your cheese of choice)
1 Tbsp Freshly Chopped Chives
4 Slices Cured Ham

Directions:

1. **Preparing the Ingredients.** Slice the fillets into four and make incisions as you would for a hamburger bun. Leave a little "hinge" uncut at the back. Season the inside and pop some brie and chives in there. Close them, and wrap them each in a slice of ham. Brush with oil and pop them into the basket.
2. **Air Frying.** Heat your fryer to 350° F. Roast the little parcels until they look tasty (15 min)

Chicken Fajitas

PREP: 10 MINUTES • COOK TIME: 10 MINUTES • TOTAL: 20 MINUTES
SERVES: 4

Ingredients

4 boneless, skinless chicken breasts, sliced
1 small red onion, sliced
2 red bell peppers, sliced
½ cup spicy ranch salad dressing, divided
½ teaspoon dried oregano
8 corn tortillas
2 cups torn butter lettuce
2 avocados, peeled and chopped

Directions:

1. **Preparing the Ingredients.** Place the chicken, onion, and pepper in the Chefman air fryer basket. Drizzle with 1 tablespoon of the salad dressing and add the oregano. Toss to combine.
2. **Air Frying.** Grill for 10 to 14 minutes or until the chicken is 165°F on a food thermometer. Transfer the chicken and vegetables to a bowl and toss with the remaining salad dressing. Serve the chicken mixture with the tortillas, lettuce, and avocados and let everyone make their own creations.

PER SERVING: CALORIES: 783; FAT: 38G; PROTEIN:72; FIBER:12G

Crispy Honey Garlic Chicken Wings

PREP: 10 MINUTES • COOK TIME: 25 MINUTES • TOTAL: 35 MINUTES
SERVES: 8

Ingredients

1/8 C. water
½ tsp. salt
4 tbsp. minced garlic
¼ C. vegan butter
¼ C. raw honey
¾ C. almond flour
16 chicken wings

Directions:

1 **Preparing the Ingredients.** Rinse off and dry chicken wings well.
Spray air fryer basket with olive oil.
Coat chicken wings with almond flour and add coated wings to air fryer.

2 **Air Frying.** Set temperature to 380°F, and set time to 25 minutes. Cook shaking every 5 minutes.
When the timer goes off, cook 5-10 minutes at 400 degrees till skin becomes crispy and dry.
As chicken cooks, melt butter in a saucepan and add garlic. Sauté garlic 5 minutes. Add salt and honey, simmering 20 minutes. Make sure to stir every so often, so the sauce does not burn. Add a bit of water after 15 minutes to ensure sauce does not harden.
Take out chicken wings from air fryer and coat in sauce. Enjoy!

 PER SERVING: CALORIES: 435; FAT: 19G; PROTEIN:31G; SUGAR:6G

BBQ Chicken Recipe from Greece

PREP: 10 MINUTES • COOK TIME: 25 MINUTES • TOTAL: 35 MINUTES
SERVES: 4

Ingredients

1 (8 ounce) container fat-free plain yogurt
2 tablespoons fresh lemon juice
2 teaspoons dried oregano
1-pound skinless, boneless chicken breast halves - cut into 1-inch pieces
1 large red onion, cut into wedges
1/2 teaspoon lemon zest
1/2 teaspoon salt
1 large green bell pepper, cut into 1 1/2-inch pieces
1/3 cup crumbled feta cheese with basil and sun-dried tomatoes
1/4 teaspoon ground black pepper
1/4 teaspoon crushed dried rosemary

Directions:

1 **Preparing the Ingredients.** In a shallow dish, mix well rosemary, pepper, salt, oregano, lemon juice, lemon zest, feta cheese, and yogurt. Add chicken and toss well to coat. Marinate in the ref for 3 hours. Thread bell pepper, onion, and chicken pieces in skewers. Place on skewer rack.

2 **Air Frying.** For 12 minutes, cook on 360°F. Halfway through cooking time, turnover skewers. If needed, cook in batches.
Serve and enjoy.

 PER SERVING: CALORIES: 242; FAT: 7.5G; PROTEIN:31G; SUGAR:6G

Chicken-Fried Steak Supreme
PREP: 10 MINUTES • COOK TIME: 30 MINUTES • TOTAL: 40 MINUTES
SERVES: 8

Ingredients
½ pound beef-bottom round, sliced into strips
1 cup of breadcrumbs (Panko brand works well)
2 medium-sized eggs
Pinch of salt and pepper
½ tablespoon of ground thyme

Directions:
1. **Preparing the Ingredients.** Cover the basket of the Chefman air fryer with a lining of tin foil, leaving the edges uncovered to allow air to circulate through the basket. Preheat the air fryer to 350 degrees. In a mixing bowl, beat the eggs until fluffy and until the yolks and whites are fully combined, and set aside. In a separate mixing bowl, combine the breadcrumbs, thyme, salt and pepper, and set aside. One by one, dip each piece of raw steak into the bowl with dry ingredients, coating all sides; then submerge into the bowl with wet ingredients, then dip again into the dry ingredients. This double coating will ensure an extra crisp air fry. Lay the coated steak pieces on the foil covering the air-fryer basket, in a single flat layer.
2. **Air Frying.** Set the Chefman air fryer timer for 15 minutes. After 15 minutes, the air fryer will turn off and the steak should be mid-way cooked and the breaded coating starting to brown. Using tongs, turn each piece of steak over to ensure a full all-over fry. Reset the air fryer to 320 degrees for 15 minutes. After 15 minutes, when the air fryer shuts off, remove the fried steak strips using tongs and set on a serving plate. Eat as soon as cool enough to handle and enjoy!

Cheesy Chicken Tenders
PREP: 10 MINUTES • COOK TIME: 30 MINUTES • TOTAL: 40 MINUTES
SERVES: 4

Ingredients
1 large white meat chicken breast, approximately 5-6 ounces, sliced into strips
1 cup of breadcrumbs (Panko brand works well)
2 medium-sized eggs
Pinch of salt and pepper
1 tablespoon of grated or powdered parmesan cheese

Directions:
1. **Preparing the Ingredients.** Cover the basket of the Chefman air fryer with a lining of tin foil, leaving the edges uncovered to allow air to circulate through the basket. Preheat the Chefman air fryer to 350 degrees. In a mixing bowl, beat the eggs until fluffy and until the yolks and whites are fully combined, and set aside. In a separate mixing bowl, combine the breadcrumbs, parmesan, salt and pepper, and set aside. One by one, dip each piece of raw chicken into the bowl with dry ingredients, coating all sides; then submerge into the bowl with wet ingredients, then dip again into the dry ingredients. Lay the coated chicken pieces on the foil covering the Chefman air fryer basket, in a single flat layer.
2. **Air Frying.** Set the Chefman air fryer timer for 15 minutes. After 15 minutes, the air fryer will turn off and the chicken should be mid-way cooked and the breaded coating starting to brown. Using tongs turn each piece of chicken over to ensure a full all over fry. Reset the air fryer to 320 degrees for another 15 minutes. After 15 minutes, when the air fryer shuts off, remove the fried chicken strips using tongs and set on a serving plate. Eat as soon as cool enough to handle, and enjoy!

PER SERVING: CALORIES: 278; FAT: 15G; PROTEIN:29G; SUGAR:7G

Lemon-Pepper Chicken Wings

PREP: 10 MINUTES • COOK TIME: 20 MINUTES • TOTAL: 30 MINUTES
SERVES: 4

PER SERVING: CALORIES: 347; FAT: 12G; PROTEIN:46G; FIBER:1G

Ingredients

8 whole chicken wings
Juice of ½ lemon
½ teaspoon garlic powder
1 teaspoon onion powder
Salt
Pepper
¼ cup low-fat buttermilk
½ cup all-purpose flour
Cooking oil

Directions:

1. **Preparing the Ingredients.** Place the wings in a sealable plastic bag. Drizzle the wings with the lemon juice. Season the wings with the garlic powder, onion powder, and salt and pepper to taste.
Seal the bag. Shake thoroughly to combine the seasonings and coat the wings.
Pour the buttermilk and the flour into separate bowls large enough to dip the wings.
Spray the Chefman air fryer basket with cooking oil.
One at a time, dip the wings in the buttermilk and then the flour.

2. **Air Frying.** Place the wings in the Chefman air fryer basket. It is okay to stack them on top of each other. Spray the wings with cooking oil, being sure to spray the bottom layer. Cook for 5 minutes.
Remove the basket and shake it to ensure all of the pieces will cook fully.
Return the basket to the Chefman air fryer and continue to cook the chicken. Repeat shaking every 5 minutes until a total of 20 minutes has passed.
Cool before serving.

Cheesy Chicken in Leek-Tomato Sauce
PREP: 10 MINUTES • COOK TIME: 20 MINUTES • TOTAL: 30 MINUTES
SERVES: 4

Ingredients
2 large-sized chicken breasts, cut in half lengthwise
Salt and ground black pepper, to taste
4 ounces Cheddar cheese, cut into sticks
1 tablespoon sesame oil
1 cup leeks, chopped
2 cloves garlic, minced
2/3 cup roasted vegetable stock
2/3 cup tomato puree
1 teaspoon dried rosemary
1 teaspoon dried thyme

Directions:
1. **Preparing the Ingredients.** Firstly, season chicken breasts with the salt and black pepper; place a piece of Cheddar cheese in the middle. Then, tie it using a kitchen string; drizzle with sesame oil and reserve.
   Add the leeks and garlic to the oven safe bowl.
2. **Air Frying.** Cook in the Chefman air fryer at 390 degrees F for 5 minutes or until tender.
   Add the reserved chicken. Throw in the other ingredients and cook for 12 to 13 minutes more or until the chicken is done. Enjoy!

Mexican Chicken Burgers
PREP: 10 MINUTES • COOK TIME: 10 MINUTES • TOTAL: 20 MINUTES
SERVES: 6

Ingredients
1 jalapeno pepper
1 tsp. cayenne pepper
1 tbsp. mustard powder
1 tbsp. oregano
1 tbsp. thyme
3 tbsp. smoked paprika
1 beaten egg
1 small head of cauliflower
4 chicken breasts

Directions:
1. **Preparing the Ingredients.** Ensure your Chefman air fryer is preheated to 350 degrees.
   Add seasonings to a blender. Slice cauliflower into florets and add to blender.
   Pulse till mixture resembles that of breadcrumbs.
   Take out ¾ of cauliflower mixture and add to a bowl. Set to the side. In another bowl, beat your egg and set to the side. Remove skin and bones from chicken breasts and add to blender with remaining cauliflower mixture. Season with pepper and salt.
   Take out mixture and form into burger shapes. Roll each patty in cauliflower crumbs, then the egg, and back into crumbs again.
2. **Air Frying.** Place coated patties into the Chefman air fryer. Set temperature to 350°F, and set time to 10 minutes.
   Flip over at 10-minute mark. They are done when crispy!

PER SERVING: CALORIES: 234; FAT: 18G; PROTEIN:24G; SUGAR:1G

Caesar Marinated Grilled Chicken

PREP: 10 MINUTES • COOK TIME: 24 MINUTES • TOTAL: 34 MINUTES
SERVES: 3

Ingredients

¼ cup crouton
1 teaspoon lemon zest. Form into ovals, skewer and grill.
1/2 cup Parmesan
1/4 cup breadcrumbs
1-pound ground chicken
2 tablespoons Caesar dressing and more for drizzling
2-4 romaine leaves

Directions:

1 **Preparing the Ingredients.** In a shallow dish, mix well chicken, 2 tablespoons Caesar dressing, parmesan, and breadcrumbs. Mix well with hands. Form into 1-inch oval patties.
    Thread chicken pieces in skewers. Place on skewer rack in air fryer.
2 **Air Frying.** For 12 minutes, cook on 360°F. Halfway through cooking time, turnover skewers. If needed, cook in batches.
    Serve and enjoy on a bed of lettuce and sprinkle with croutons and extra dressing.

PER SERVING: CALORIES: 339; FAT: 18.9G; PROTEIN:32.6G; SUGAR:1G

Minty Chicken-Fried Pork Chops

PREP: 10 MINUTES • COOK TIME: 30 MINUTES • TOTAL: 40 MINUTES
SERVES: 6

Ingredients

4 medium-sized pork chops, approximately 3.5 ounces each
1 cup of breadcrumbs (Panko brand works well)
2 medium-sized eggs
Pinch of salt and pepper
½ tablespoon of mint, either dried and ground; or fresh, rinsed, and finely chopped

Directions:

1. **Preparing the Ingredients.** Cover the basket of the Chefman air fryer with a lining of tin foil, leaving the edges uncovered to allow air to circulate through the basket. Preheat the Chefman air fryer to 350 degrees.
   In a mixing bowl, beat the eggs until fluffy and until the yolks and whites are fully combined, and set aside.
   In a separate mixing bowl, combine the breadcrumbs, mint, salt and pepper, and set aside. One by one, dip each raw pork chop into the bowl with dry ingredients, coating all sides; then submerge into the bowl with wet ingredients, then dip again into the dry ingredients. This double coating will ensure an extra crisp air-fry. Lay the coated pork chops on the foil covering the Chefman air fryer basket, in a single flat layer.
2. **Air Frying.** Set the Chefman air fryer timer for 15 minutes. After 15 minutes, the Chefman air fryer will turn off and the pork should be mid-way cooked and the breaded coating starting to brown. Using tongs, turn each piece of steak over to ensure a full all-over fry. Reset the air fryer to 320 degrees for 15 minutes. After 15 minutes, when the air fryer shuts off, remove the fried pork chops using tongs and set on a serving plate. Eat as soon as cool enough to handle – and enjoy!

Fried Chicken Livers

PREP: 5 MINUTES • COOK TIME: 10 MINUTES • TOTAL: 15 MINUTES
SERVES: 4

Ingredients

1 pound chicken livers
1 cup flour
1/2 cup cornmeal
2 teaspoons your favorite seasoning blend
3 eggs
2 tablespoons milk

Directions:

1. **Preparing the Ingredients.** Clean and rinse the livers, pat dry.
   Beat eggs in a shallow bowl and mix in milk.
   In another bowl combine flour, cornmeal, and seasoning, mixing until even.
   Dip the livers in the egg mix, then toss them in the flour mix.
2. **Air Frying.** Air-fry at 375 degrees for 10 minutes using your Chefman air fryer. Toss at least once halfway through.

PER SERVING: CALORIES: 409; FAT: 11G; PROTEIN:36G; FIBER:2G

Fried Chicken Sandwich

PREP: 10 MINUTES • COOK TIME: 15 MINUTES • TOTAL: 25 MINUTES
SERVES: 4

Ingredients

4 small skinless, boneless chicken thighs
3/4 cups low-fat buttermilk
2 teaspoons garlic powder
1/2 teaspoon salt
1/2 teaspoon pepper
1 cup all-purpose flour
4 potato rolls
Shredded romaine
Sliced tomatoes
Sliced pickles
Hot sauce

Directions:

1. **Preparing the Ingredients.** Place your chicken in a large bowl and mix in buttermilk, garlic powder, salt, and pepper.
   Place the flour in a separate bowl.
   Pull the chicken out of the buttermilk mix, letting excess drip off, cover in flour, dip in buttermilk mix, then cover in flour again.
2. **Air Frying.** Using your Chefman air fryer, cook at 360 degrees for 15 minutes, flipping the chicken halfway through.
   Serve on a potato roll with lettuce, tomatoes, pickles, and hot sauce.

PER SERVING: CALORIES: 393; FAT: 4,4G; PROTEIN:31G; FIBER:4.8G

Crispy Southern Fried Chicken

PREP: 10 MINUTES • COOK TIME: 25 MINUTES • TOTAL: 35 MINUTES SERVES: 4

Ingredients

1 tsp. cayenne pepper
2 tbsp. mustard powder
2 tbsp. oregano
2 tbsp. thyme
3 tbsp. coconut milk
1 beaten egg
¼ C. cauliflower
¼ C. gluten-free oats
8 chicken drumsticks

Directions:

1 **Preparing the Ingredients.** Ensure the Chefman air fryer is preheated to 350 degrees.
Lay out chicken and season with pepper and salt on all sides.
Add all other ingredients to a blender, blending till a smooth-like breadcrumb mixture is created. Place in a bowl and add a beaten egg to another bowl.
Dip chicken into breadcrumbs, then into egg, and breadcrumbs once more.

2 **Air Frying.** Place coated drumsticks into the Chefman air fryer. Set temperature to 350°F, and set time to 20 minutes and cook 20 minutes. Bump up the temperature to 390 degrees and cook another 5 minutes till crispy.

PER SERVING: CALORIES: 504; FAT: 18G; PROTEIN:35G; SUGAR:5G

Chicken Roast with Pineapple Salsa

PREP: 10 MINUTES • COOK TIME: 45 MINUTES • TOTAL: 55 MINUTES SERVES: 2

Ingredients

¼ cup extra virgin olive oil
¼ cup freshly chopped cilantro
1 avocado, diced
1-pound boneless chicken breasts
2 cups canned pineapples
2 teaspoons honey
Juice from 1 lime
Salt and pepper to taste

Directions:

1 **Preparing the Ingredients.** Preheat the air fryer to 390°F.
Place the grill pan accessory in the air fryer.
Season the chicken breasts with lime juice, olive oil, honey, salt, and pepper.

2 **Air Frying.** Place on the grill pan and cook for 45 minutes.
Flip the chicken every 10 minutes to grill all sides evenly.
Once the chicken is cooked, serve with pineapples, cilantro, and avocado.

PER SERVING: CALORIES: 744; FAT: 32.8G; PROTEIN:4.7G; SUGAR:5G

Tex-Mex Turkey Burgers

PREP: 10 MINUTES • COOK TIME: 15 MINUTES • TOTAL: 25 MINUTES
SERVES: 4

Ingredients
⅓ cup finely crushed corn tortilla chips
1 egg, beaten
¼ cup salsa
⅓ cup shredded pepper Jack cheese
Pinch salt
Freshly ground black pepper
1 pound ground turkey
1 tablespoon olive oil
1 teaspoon paprika

Directions:
1. **Preparing the Ingredients.** In a medium bowl, combine the tortilla chips, egg, salsa, cheese, salt, and pepper, and mix well.
   Add the turkey and mix gently but thoroughly with clean hands.
   Form the meat mixture into patties about ½ inch thick. Make an indentation in the center of each patty with your thumb so the burgers don't puff up while cooking.
   Brush the patties on both sides with the olive oil and sprinkle with paprika.
2. **Air Frying.** Put in the Chefman air fryer basket. Grill for 14 to 16 minutes or until the meat registers at least 165°F.

PER SERVING: CALORIES: 354; FAT: 21G; PROTEIN:36G; FIBER:2G

Air Fryer Turkey Breast

PREP: 5 MINUTES • COOK TIME: 60 MINUTES • TOTAL: 65 MINUTES
SERVES: 6

Ingredients
Pepper and salt
1 oven-ready turkey breast
Turkey seasonings of choice

Directions:
1. **Preparing the Ingredients.** Preheat the Chefman air fryer to 350 degrees.
   Season turkey with pepper, salt, and other desired seasonings.
   Place turkey in air fryer basket.
2. **Air Frying.** Set temperature to 350°F, and set time to 60 minutes. Cook 60 minutes. The meat should be at 165 degrees when done.
   Allow to rest 10-15 minutes before slicing. Enjoy!

PER SERVING: CALORIES: 212; FAT: 12G; PROTEIN:24G; SUGAR:0G

Cheese Stuffed Chicken

PREP: 5 MINUTES • COOK TIME: 30 MINUTES • TOTAL: 35 MINUTES
SERVES: 4

Ingredients

1 tablespoon creole seasoning
1 tablespoon olive oil
1 teaspoon garlic powder
1 teaspoon onion powder
4 chicken breasts, butterflied and pounded
4 slices Colby cheese
4 slices pepper jack cheese

Directions:

1 **Preparing the Ingredients.** Preheat the air fryer to 390°F.

Place the grill pan accessory in the air fryer.

Create the dry rub by mixing in a bowl the creole seasoning, garlic powder, and onion powder. Season with salt and pepper if desired.

Rub the seasoning on to the chicken.

Place the chicken on a working surface and place a slice each of pepper jack and Colby cheese.

Fold the chicken and secure the edges with toothpicks.

Brush chicken with olive oil.

2 **Air Frying.** Grill for 30 minutes and make sure to flip the meat every 10 minutes.

PER SERVING: CALORIES: 27; FAT: 45.9G; PROTEIN:73.1G; SUGAR:0G

Orange Curried Chicken Stir-Fry

PREP: 10 MINUTES • COOK TIME: 18 MINUTES • TOTAL: 28 MINUTES
SERVES: 4

Ingredients

¾ pound boneless, skinless chicken thighs, cut into 1-inch pieces
1 yellow bell pepper, cut into 1½-inch pieces
1 small red onion, sliced
Olive oil for misting
¼ cup chicken stock
2 tablespoons honey
¼ cup orange juice
1 tablespoon cornstarch
3 to 3 teaspoons curry powder

Directions:

1. **Preparing the Ingredients.** Put the chicken thighs, pepper, and red onion in the Chefman air fryer basket and mist with olive oil.

2. **Air Frying.** Cook for 12 to 14 minutes or until the chicken is cooked to 165°F, shaking the basket halfway through cooking time.

Remove the chicken and vegetables from the air fryer basket and set aside.

In a 6-inch metal bowl, combine the stock, honey, orange juice, cornstarch, and curry powder, and mix well. Add the chicken and vegetables, stir, and put the bowl in the basket.

Return the basket to the Chefman air fryer and cook for 2 minutes. Remove and stir, then cook for 2 to 3 minutes or until the sauce is thickened and bubbly.

PER SERVING: CALORIES: 230; FAT: 7G; PROTEIN:26G; FIBER:2G

Mustard Chicken Tenders

PREP: 5 MINUTES • COOK TIME: 20 MINUTES • TOTAL: 25 MINUTES
SERVES: 4

Ingredients
½ C. coconut flour
1 tbsp. spicy brown mustard
2 beaten eggs
1 pound of chicken tenders

Directions:
1 **Preparing the Ingredients.** Season tenders with pepper and salt.
Place a thin layer of mustard onto tenders and then dredge in flour and dip in egg.
2 **Air Frying.** Add to the Chefman air fryer, set temperature to 390°F, and set time to 20 minutes.

PER SERVING: CALORIES: 403; FAT: 20G; PROTEIN:22G; SUGAR:4G

Chicken Pot Pie with Coconut Milk

Se PREP: 5 MINUTES • COOK TIME: 30 MINUTES • TOTAL: 40 MINUTES
SERVES: 8

Ingredients
¼ small onion, chopped
½ cup broccoli, chopped
¾ cup coconut milk
1 cup chicken broth
1/3 cup coconut flour
1-pound ground chicken
2 cloves of garlic, minced
2 tablespoons butter
4 ½ tablespoons butter, melted
4 eggs
Salt and pepper to taste

Directions:
1 **Preparing the Ingredients.** Preheat the air fryer for 5 minutes.
Place 2 tablespoons butter, broccoli, onion, garlic, coconut milk, chicken broth, and ground chicken in a baking dish that will fit in the air fryer. Season with salt and pepper to taste.
In a mixing bowl, combine the butter, coconut flour, and eggs.
Sprinkle evenly the top of the chicken and broccoli mixture with the coconut flour dough.
Place the dish in the air fryer.
2 **Air Frying.** Cook for 30 minutes at 325°F.

PER SERVING: CALORIES: 366; FAT: 29.5G; PROTEIN:21.8G; SUGAR:4G

Chicken Nuggets

PREP: 10 MINUTES • COOK TIME: 20 MINUTES • TOTAL: 30 MINUTES SERVES: 4

Ingredients

1 pound boneless, skinless chicken breasts
Chicken seasoning or rub
Salt
Pepper
2 eggs
6 tablespoons bread crumbs
2 tablespoons panko bread crumbs
Cooking oil

Directions:

1. **Preparing the Ingredients.** Cut the chicken breasts into 1-inch pieces.
   In a large bowl, combine the chicken pieces with chicken seasoning, salt, and pepper to taste.
   In a small bowl, beat the eggs. In another bowl, combine the bread crumbs and panko.
   Dip the chicken pieces in the eggs and then the bread crumbs.
   Place the nuggets in the Chefman air fryer. Do not overcrowd the basket. Cook in batches. Spray the nuggets with cooking oil.
2. **Air Frying.** Cook for 4 minutes. Open the Chefman air fryer and shake the basket. Cook for an additional 4 minutes. Remove the cooked nuggets from the Chefman air fryer, then repeat steps 5 and 6 for the remaining chicken nuggets. Cool before serving.

PER SERVING: CALORIES: 206; FAT: 5G; PROTEIN:31G; FIBER:1G

Cheesy Chicken Fritters

PREP: 5 MINUTES • COOK TIME: 20 MINUTES • TOTAL: 25 MINUTES SERVES: 17 FRITTERS

Ingredients

Chicken Fritters:
½ tsp. salt
1/8 tsp. pepper
1 ½ tbsp. fresh dill
1 1/3 C. shredded mozzarella cheese
1/3 C. coconut flour
1/3 C. vegan mayo
2 eggs
1 ½ pounds chicken breasts
Garlic Dip:
1/8 tsp. pepper
¼ tsp. salt
½ tbsp. lemon juice
1 pressed garlic cloves
1/3 C. vegan mayo

Directions:

1. **Preparing the Ingredients.** Slice chicken breasts into 1/3" pieces and place in a bowl. Add all remaining fritter ingredients to the bowl and stir well. Cover and chill 2 hours or overnight.
   Ensure your air fryer is preheated to 350 degrees. Spray basket with a bit of olive oil.
2. **Air Frying.** Add marinated chicken to air fryer. Set temperature to 350°F, and set time to 20 minutes and cook 20 minutes, making sure to turn halfway through cooking process.
   To make the dipping sauce, combine all the dip ingredients until smooth.

PER SERVING: CALORIES: 467; FAT: 27G; PROTEIN:21G; SUGAR:3G

Chicken BBQ with Sweet And Sour Sauce

PREP: 5 MINUTES • COOK TIME: 40 MINUTES • TOTAL: 45 MINUTES
SERVES: 6

Ingredients

¼ cup minced garlic
¼ cup tomato paste
¾ cup minced onion
¾ cup sugar
1 cup soy sauce
1 cup water
1 cup white vinegar
6 chicken drumsticks
Salt and pepper to taste

Directions:

1 **Preparing the Ingredients.** Place all Ingredients in a Ziploc bag
   Allow to marinate for at least 2 hours in the fridge.
   Preheat the air fryer to 390°F.
   Place the grill pan accessory in the air fryer.
2 **Air Frying.** Grill the chicken for 40 minutes.
   Flip the chicken every 10 minutes for even grilling.
   Meanwhile, pour the marinade in a saucepan and heat over medium flame until the sauce thickens.
   Before serving the chicken, brush with the glaze.

PER SERVING: CALORIES: 4607; FAT: 19.7G; PROTEIN:27.8G; SUGAR:3G

Thai Basll Chicken

PREP: 5 MINUTES • COOK TIME: 20 MINUTES • TOTAL: 25 MINUTES
SERVES: 4

Ingredients

 4 Chicken Breasts
1 Onion
2 Bell Peppers
2 Hot Peppers
1 Tbsp Olive Oil
3 Tbsps Fish Sauce
2 Tbsps Oyster Sauce
3 Tbsps Sweet Chili Sauce
1 Tbsp Soy Sauce
1 Quart Chicken Broth
1 Tbsp Garlic Powder
1 Tbsp Chili Powder
1 Cup Thai Basil

Directions:

1 **Preparing the Ingredients.** Wash the breasts and boil them in the chicken broth for 10 minutes, then lower to simmer for another 10 minutes until tender. Take them out of the broth and allow to cool
   Using two forks, tear the chicken into shreds. Toss the shreds with the garlic powder, chili powder, and salt and pepper to taste
2 **Air Frying.** Preheat the Chefman air fryer to 390 degrees and cook the chicken shreds for 20 minutes, at which point they will get dark brown and crispy. They will soften up as they absorb the juices from cooking with the veggies
   While the chicken is cooking, cut the onions and peppers into thin slices. Add the olive oil to a wok and heat for a minute on medium high heat. Toss in all the veggies and sauté for 5 minutes

Add in the fish sauce, oyster sauce, soy sauce, sweet chili sauce, and stir well for 1 minute. Add the chicken and basil leaves and stir until the leaves have wilted Serve over jasmine rice.

PER SERVING: CALORIES: 351; FAT: 14G; PROTEIN:23G; SUGAR:2G

Crusted Chicken Tenders

PREP: 5 MINUTES • COOK TIME: 15 MINUTES • TOTAL: 20 MINUTES SERVES: 3

Ingredients
½ cup all-purpose flour
2 eggs, beaten
½ cup seasoned breadcrumbs
Salt and freshly ground black pepper, to taste
2 tablespoons olive oil
¾ pound chicken tenders

Directions:

1 **Preparing the Ingredients.** In a bowl, place the flour.
   In a second bowl, place the eggs.
   In a third bowl, mix together breadcrumbs, salt, black pepper and oil.
   Coat the chicken tenders in the flour,
   Then dip into the eggs and finally coat with the breadcrumbs mixture evenly.
2 **Air Frying.** Preheat the Chefman air fryer to 330 degrees F. Arrange the chicken tenderloins in Air fryer basket. Cook for about 10 minutes.
   Now, set the Air fryer to 390 degrees F.
   Cook for about 5 minutes further.

Air Fryer Chicken Parmesan

PREP: 5 MINUTES • COOK TIME: 9 MINUTES • TOTAL: 20 MINUTES
SERVES: 4

Ingredients

½ C. keto marinara
6 tbsp. mozzarella cheese
1 tbsp. melted ghee
2 tbsp. grated parmesan cheese
6 tbsp. gluten-free seasoned breadcrumbs
1   8-ounce chicken breasts

Directions:

1 **Preparing the Ingredients.** Ensure air fryer is preheated to 360 degrees. Spray the basket with olive oil.
   Mix parmesan cheese and breadcrumbs together. Melt ghee.
   Brush melted ghee onto the chicken and dip into breadcrumb mixture.
   Place coated chicken in the air fryer and top with olive oil.

2 **Air Frying.** Set temperature to 360°F, and set time to 6 minutes. Cook 2 breasts for 6 minutes and top each breast with a tablespoon of sauce and 1½ tablespoons of mozzarella cheese. Cook another 3 minutes to melt cheese.
   Keep cooked pieces warm as you repeat the process with remaining breasts.

PER SERVING: CALORIES: 251; FAT: 10G; PROTEIN:31G; SUGAR:0G

Chicken BBQ Recipe from Peru

PREP: 5 MINUTES • COOK TIME: 40 MINUTES • TOTAL: 45 MINUTES
SERVES: 4

Ingredients

½ teaspoon dried oregano
1 teaspoon paprika
1/3 cup soy sauce
2 ½ pounds chicken, quartered
2 tablespoons fresh lime juice
2 teaspoons ground cumin
5 cloves of garlic, minced

Directions:

1 **Preparing the Ingredients.** Place all Ingredients in a Ziploc bag and shake to mix everything.
   Allow to marinate for at least 2 hours in the fridge.
   Preheat the air fryer to 390°F.
   Place the grill pan accessory in the air fryer.

2 **Air Frying** Grill the chicken for 40 minutes making sure to flip the chicken every 10 minutes for even grilling.

PER SERVING: CALORIES: 377; FAT: 11.8G; PROTEIN:59.7G; SUGAR:0G

Ricotta and Parsley Stuffed Turkey Breasts

PREP: 5 MINUTES • COOK TIME: 25 MINUTES • TOTAL: 30 MINUTES

SERVES: 4

Ingredients

1 turkey breast, quartered
1 cup Ricotta cheese
1/4 cup fresh Italian parsley, chopped
1 teaspoon garlic powder
1/2 teaspoon cumin powder
1 egg, beaten
1 teaspoon paprika
Salt and ground black pepper, to taste
Crushed tortilla chips
1 ½ tablespoons extra-virgin olive oil

Directions:

1 **Preparing the Ingredients.** Firstly, flatten out each piece of turkey breast with a rolling pin. Prepare three mixing bowls.
   In a shallow bowl, combine Ricotta cheese with the parsley, garlic powder, and cumin powder.
   Place the Ricotta/parsley mixture in the middle of each piece. Repeat with the remaining pieces of the turkey breast and roll them up.
   In another shallow bowl, whisk the egg together with paprika. In the third shallow bowl, combine the salt, pepper, and crushed tortilla chips.
   Dip each roll in the whisked egg, then, roll them over the tortilla chips mixture.
   Transfer prepared rolls to the Chefman air fryer basket. Drizzle olive oil over all.
2 **Air Frying.** Cook at 350 degrees F for 25 minutes, working in batches. Serve warm, garnished with some extra parsley, if desired.

Cheesy Turkey-Rice with Broccoli

PREP: 5 MINUTES • COOK TIME: 40 MINUTES • TOTAL: 45 MINUTES

SERVES: 4

Ingredients

1 cup cooked, chopped turkey meat
1 tablespoon and 1-1/2 teaspoons butter, melted
1/2 (10 ounce) package frozen broccoli, thawed
1/2 (7 ounce) package whole wheat crackers, crushed
1/2 cup shredded Cheddar cheese
1/2 cup uncooked white rice

Directions:

1 **Preparing the Ingredients.** Bring to a boil 2 cups of water in a saucepan. Stir in rice and simmer for 20 minutes. Turn off fire and set aside.
   Lightly grease baking pan of air fryer with cooking spray. Mix in cooked rice, cheese, broccoli, and turkey. Toss well to mix.
   Mix well melted butter and crushed crackers in a small bowl. Evenly spread on top of rice.
2 **Air Frying.** For 20 minutes, cook on 360°F until tops are lightly browned.
   Serve and enjoy.

PER SERVING: CALORIES: 269; FAT: 11.8G; PROTEIN:17G; SUGAR:0G

Jerk Chicken Wings

PREP: 10 MINUTES • COOK TIME: 16 MINUTES • TOTAL: 26 MINUTES
SERVES: 6

Ingredients
1 tsp. salt
½ C. red wine vinegar
5 tbsp. lime juice
4 chopped scallions
1 tbsp. grated ginger
2 tbsp. brown sugar
1 tbsp. chopped thyme
1 tsp. white pepper
1 tsp. cayenne pepper
1 tsp. cinnamon
1 tbsp. allspice
1 Habanero pepper (seeds/ribs removed and chopped finely)
6 chopped garlic cloves
2 tbsp. low-sodium soy sauce
2 tbsp. olive oil
4 pounds of chicken wings

Directions:

1 **Preparing the Ingredients.** Combine all ingredients except wings in a bowl. Pour into a gallon bag and add chicken wings. Chill 2-24 hours to marinate.
Ensure your air fryer is preheated to 390 degrees.
Place chicken wings into a strainer to drain excess liquids.

2 **Air Frying.** Pour half of the wings into your Chefman air fryer. Set temperature to 390°F, and set time to 16 minutes and cook 14-16 minutes, making sure to shake halfway through the cooking process. Remove and repeat the process with remaining wings.

PER SERVING: CALORIES: 374; FAT: 14G; PROTEIN:33G; SUGAR:4G

56

Pork Taquitos

PREP: 10 MINUTES • COOK TIME: 16 MINUTES • TOTAL: 26 MINUTES
SERVES: 8

Ingredients
1 juiced lime
10 whole wheat tortillas
2 ½ C. shredded mozzarella cheese
30 ounces of cooked and shredded pork tenderloin

Directions:
1 **Preparing the Ingredients**. Ensure your air fryer is preheated to 380 degrees.
Drizzle pork with lime juice and gently mix.
Heat up tortillas in the microwave with a dampened paper towel to soften.
Add about 3 ounces of pork and ¼ cup of shredded cheese to each tortilla. Tightly roll them up.
Spray the Chefman air fryer basket with a bit of olive oil.
2 **Air Frying**. Set temperature to 380°F, and set time to 10 minutes. Air fry taquitos 7-10 minutes till tortillas turn a slight golden color, making sure to flip halfway through cooking process.

PER SERVING: CALORIES: 309; FAT: 11G; PROTEIN:21G; SUGAR:2G

Panko-Breaded Pork Chops

PREP: 5 MINUTES • COOK TIME: 12 MINUTES • TOTAL: 17 MINUTES
SERVES: 6

Ingredients
5 (3½- to 5-ounce) pork chops (bone-in or boneless)
Seasoning salt
Pepper
¼ cup all-purpose flour
2 tablespoons panko bread crumbs
Cooking oil

Directions:
1. **Preparing the Ingredients.** Season the pork chops with the seasoning salt and pepper to taste.
Sprinkle the flour on both sides of the pork chops, then coat both sides with panko bread crumbs.
Place the pork chops in the air fryer. Stacking them is okay.
2. **Air Frying.** Spray the pork chops with cooking oil. Cook for 6 minutes.
Open the Chefman air fryer and flip the pork chops. Cook for an additional 6 minutes
Cool before serving.
Typically, bone-in pork chops are juicier than boneless. If you prefer really juicy pork chops, use bone-in.

PER SERVING: CALORIES: 246; FAT: 13G; PROTEIN:26G; FIBER:0G

Apricot Glazed Pork Tenderloins

PREP: 5 MINUTES • COOK TIME: 30 MINUTES • TOTAL: 35 MINUTES
SERVES: 3

Ingredients
1 teaspoon salt
1/2 teaspoon pepper
1-lb pork tenderloin
2 tablespoons minced fresh rosemary or 1 tablespoon dried rosemary, crushed
2 tablespoons olive oil, divided
3   garlic cloves, minced

Apricot Glaze Ingredients
1 cup apricot preserves
3   garlic cloves, minced
4 tablespoons lemon juice

Directions:
1 **Preparing the Ingredients.** Mix well pepper, salt, garlic, oil, and rosemary. Brush all over pork. If needed cut pork crosswise in half to fit in air fryer.
Lightly grease baking pan of air fryer with cooking spray. Add pork.
2 **Air Frying.** For 3 minutes per side, brown pork in a preheated 390°F air fryer.
Meanwhile, mix well all glaze Ingredients in a small bowl. Baste pork every 5 minutes.
Cook for 20 minutes at 330°F.
Serve and enjoy.

PER SERVING: CALORIES: 281; FAT: 9G; PROTEIN:23G; FIBER:0G

Pork Tenders With Bell Peppers

PREP: 5 MINUTES • COOK TIME: 15 MINUTES • TOTAL: 20 MINUTES
SERVES: 4

Ingredients
11 Ozs Pork Tenderloin
1 Bell Pepper, in thin strips
1 Red Onion, sliced
2 Tsps Provencal Herbs
Black Pepper to taste
1 Tbsp Olive Oil
1/2 Tbsp Mustard
* Round Oven Dish

Directions:
1. **Preparing the Ingredients.** Preheat the Chefman air fryer to 390 degrees.
In the oven dish, mix the bell pepper strips with the onion, herbs, and some salt and pepper to taste.
Add half a tablespoon of olive oil to the mixture
Cut the pork tenderloin into four pieces and rub with salt, pepper and mustard.
Thinly coat the pieces with remaining olive oil and place them upright in the oven dish on top of the pepper mixture
2. **Air Frying.** Place the bowl into the Chefman air fryer. Set the timer to 15 minutes and roast the meat and the vegetables
Turn the meat and mix the peppers halfway through
Serve with a fresh salad

Barbecue Flavored Pork Ribs

PREP: 5 MINUTES • COOK TIME: 15 MINUTES • TOTAL: 25 MINUTES
SERVES: 6

Ingredients
¼ cup honey, divided
¾ cup BBQ sauce
2 tablespoons tomato ketchup
1 tablespoon Worcestershire sauce
1 tablespoon soy sauce
½ teaspoon garlic powder
Freshly ground white pepper, to taste
1¾ pound pork ribs

Directions:
1. **Preparing the Ingredients.** In a large bowl, mix together 3 tablespoons of honey and remaining ingredients except pork ribs.
   Refrigerate to marinate for about 20 minutes.
   Preheat the Chefman air fryer to 355 degrees F.
   Place the ribs in an Air fryer basket.
2. **Air Frying.** Cook for about 13 minutes.
   Remove the ribs from the Chefman air fryer and coat with remaining honey.
   Serve hot.

Balsamic Glazed Pork Chops

PREP: 5 MINUTES • COOK TIME: 50 MINUTES • TOTAL: 55 MINUTES
SERVES: 4

Ingredients
¾ cup balsamic vinegar
1 ½ tablespoons sugar
1 tablespoon butter
3 tablespoons olive oil
3   tablespoons salt
3 pork rib chops

Directions:
1. **Preparing the Ingredients.** Place all ingredients in bowl and allow the meat to marinate in the fridge for at least 2 hours.
   Preheat the air fryer to 390°F.
   Place the grill pan accessory in the air fryer.
2. **Air Frying.** Grill the pork chops for 20 minutes making sure to flip the meat every 10 minutes for even grilling.
   Meanwhile, pour the balsamic vinegar on a saucepan and allow to simmer for at least 10 minutes until the sauce thickens.
   Brush the meat with the glaze before serving.

PER SERVING: CALORIES: 274; FAT: 18G; PROTEIN:17G

Rustic Pork Ribs

PREP: 5 MINUTES • COOK TIME: 15 MINUTES • TOTAL: 25 MINUTES
SERVES: 4

Ingredients

1 rack of pork ribs
3 tablespoons dry red wine
1 tablespoon soy sauce
1/2 teaspoon dried thyme
1/2 teaspoon onion powder
1/2 teaspoon garlic powder
1/2 teaspoon ground black pepper
1 teaspoon smoke salt
1 tablespoon cornstarch
1/2 teaspoon olive oil

Directions:

1. **Preparing the Ingredients.** Begin by preheating your Chefman air fryer to 390 degrees F. Place all ingredients in a mixing bowl and let them marinate at least 1 hour.
2. **Air Frying.** Cook the marinated ribs approximately 25 minutes at 390 degrees F.
   Serve hot.

Keto Parmesan Crusted Pork Chops

PREP: 10 MINUTES • COOK TIME: 15 MINUTES • TOTAL: 25 MINUTES
SERVES: 8

Ingredients

3 tbsp. grated parmesan cheese
1 C. pork rind crumbs
2 beaten eggs
¼ tsp. chili powder
½ tsp. onion powder
1 tsp. smoked paprika
¼ tsp. pepper
½ tsp. salt
4-6 thick boneless pork chops

Directions:

1. **Preparing the Ingredients.** Ensure your air fryer is preheated to 400 degrees.
   With pepper and salt, season both sides of pork chops.
   In a food processor, pulse pork rinds into crumbs. Mix crumbs with other seasonings.
   Beat eggs and add to another bowl.
   Dip pork chops into eggs then into pork rind crumb mixture.
2. **Air Frying.** Spray down air fryer with olive oil and add pork chops to the basket. Set temperature to 400°F, and set time to 15 minutes.

PER SERVING: CALORIES: 422; FAT: 19G; PROTEIN:38G; SUGAR:2G

Crispy Fried Pork Chops the Southern Way

PREP: 10 MINUTES • COOK TIME: 25 MINUTES • TOTAL: 35 MINUTES
SERVES: 4

Ingredients
½ cup all-purpose flour
½ cup low fat buttermilk
½ teaspoon black pepper
½ teaspoon Tabasco sauce
teaspoon paprika
3 bone-in pork chops

Directions:
1 **Preparing the Ingredients.** Place the buttermilk and hot sauce in a Ziploc bag and add the pork chops. Allow to marinate for at least an hour in the fridge.
In a bowl, combine the flour, paprika, and black pepper.
Remove pork from the Ziploc bag and dredge in the flour mixture.
Preheat the air fryer to 390°F.
Spray the pork chops with cooking oil.
2 **Air Frying.** Place in the air fryer basket and cook for 25 minutes.

PER SERVING: CALORIES: 427; FAT: 21.2G; PROTEIN:46.4G; SUGAR:2G

Fried Pork Quesadilla

PREP: 10 MINUTES • COOK TIME: 12 MINUTES • TOTAL: 22 MINUTES
SERVES: 2

Ingredients
Two 6-inch corn or flour tortilla shells
1 medium-sized pork shoulder, approximately 4 ounces, sliced
½ medium-sized white onion, sliced
½ medium-sized red pepper, sliced
½ medium sized green pepper, sliced
½ medium sized yellow pepper, sliced
¼ cup of shredded pepper-jack cheese
¼ cup of shredded mozzarella cheese

Directions:
1. **Preparing the Ingredients.** Preheat the Chefman air fryer to 350 degrees.
In the oven on high heat for 20 minutes, grill the pork, onion, and peppers in foil in the same pan, allowing the moisture from the vegetables and the juice from the pork mingle together. Remove pork and vegetables in foil from the oven. While they're cooling, sprinkle half the shredded cheese over one of the tortillas, then cover with the pieces of pork, onions, and peppers, and then layer on the rest of the shredded cheese. Top with the second tortilla. Place directly on hot surface of the Chefman air fryer basket.
2. **Air Frying.** Set the Chefman air fryer timer for 6 minutes. After 6 minutes, when the Chefman air fryer shuts off, flip the tortillas onto the other side with a spatula; the cheese should be melted enough that it won't fall apart, but be careful anyway not to spill any toppings!
Reset the Chefman air fryer to 350 degrees for another 6 minutes.
After 6 minutes, when the air fryer shuts off, the tortillas should be browned and

crisp, and the pork, onion, peppers and cheese will be crispy and hot and delicious. Remove with tongs and let sit on a serving plate to cool for a few minutes before slicing.

Pork Wonton Wonderful

PREP: 10 MINUTES • COOK TIME: 25 MINUTES • TOTAL: 35 MINUTES
SERVES: 3

Ingredients

8 wanton wrappers (Leasa brand works great, though any will do)
4 ounces of raw minced pork
1 medium-sized green apple
1 cup of water, for wetting the wanton wrappers
1 tablespoon of vegetable oil
½ tablespoon of oyster sauce
1 tablespoon of soy sauce
Large pinch of ground white pepper

Directions:

1. **Preparing the Ingredients.** Cover the basket of the Chefman air fryer with a lining of tin foil, leaving the edges uncovered to allow air to circulate through the basket. Preheat the air fryer to 350 degrees.

    In a small mixing bowl, combine the oyster sauce, soy sauce, and white pepper, then add in the minced pork and stir thoroughly. Cover and set in the fridge to marinate for at least 15 minutes. Core the apple, and slice into small cubes – smaller than bite-sized chunks.

    Add the apples to the marinating meat mixture, and combine thoroughly. Spread the wonton wrappers, and fill each with a large spoonful of the filling. Wrap the wontons into triangles, so that the wrappers fully cover the filling, and seal with a drop of the water.

    Coat each filled and wrapped wonton thoroughly with the vegetable oil, to help ensure a nice crispy fry. Place the wontons on the foil-lined air-fryer basket.

2. **Air Frying.** Set the Chefman air fryer timer to 25 minutes. Halfway through cooking time, shake the handle of the air fryer basket vigorously to jostle the wontons and ensure even frying. After 25 minutes, when the Chefman air fryer shuts off, the wontons will be crispy golden-brown on the outside and juicy and delicious on the inside. Serve directly from the Chefman air fryer basket and enjoy while hot.

Cilantro-Mint Pork BBQ Thai Style
PREP: 5 MINUTES • COOK TIME: 15 MINUTES • TOTAL: 20 MINUTES
SERVES: 3

Ingredients
1 minced hot chile
1 minced shallot
1-pound ground pork
2 tablespoons fish sauce
2 tablespoons lime juice
3 tablespoons basil
3   tablespoons chopped mint
3 tablespoons cilantro

Directions:
1 **Preparing the Ingredients.** In a shallow dish, mix well all Ingredients with hands. Form into 1-inch ovals.
   Thread ovals in skewers. Place on skewer rack in air fryer.
2 **Air Frying** For 15 minutes, cook on 360°F. Halfway through cooking time, turnover skewers. If needed, cook in batches.
   Serve and enjoy.

PER SERVING: CALORIES: 455; FAT: 31.5G; PROTEIN:40.4G

Tuscan Pork Chops

PREP: 10 MINUTES • COOK TIME: 10 MINUTES • TOTAL: 20 MINUTES
SERVES: 4

Ingredients

1/4 cup all-purpose flour
1 teaspoon salt
3/4 teaspoons seasoned pepper
4 (1-inch-thick) boneless pork chops
1 tablespoon olive oil
3 to 4 garlic cloves
1/3 cup balsamic vinegar
1/3 cup chicken broth
3 plum tomatoes, seeded and diced
3 tablespoons capers

Directions:

1. **Preparing the Ingredients.** Combine flour, salt, and pepper
   Press pork chops into flour mixture on both sides until evenly covered.
2. **Air Frying.** Cook in your Chefman air fryer at 360 degrees for 14 minutes, flipping half way through.
   While the pork chops cook, warm olive oil in a medium skillet.
   Add garlic and sauté for 1 minute; then mix in vinegar and chicken broth.
   Add capers and tomatoes and turn to high heat.
   Bring the sauce to a boil, stirring regularly, then add pork chops, cooking for one minute.
   Remove from heat and cover for about 5 minutes to allow the pork to absorb some of the sauce; serve hot.

PER SERVING: CALORIES: 349; FAT: 23G; PROTEIN:20G; FIBER:1.5G

Italian Parmesan Breaded Pork Chops

PREP: 5 MINUTES • COOK TIME: 25 MINUTES • TOTAL: 30 MINUTES
SERVES: 5

Ingredients

5 (3½- to 5-ounce) pork chops (bone-in or boneless)
1 teaspoon Italian seasoning
Seasoning salt
Pepper
¼ cup all-purpose flour
2 tablespoons Italian bread crumbs
3 tablespoons finely grated Parmesan cheese
Cooking oil

Directions:

1. **Preparing the Ingredients.** Season the pork chops with the Italian seasoning and seasoning salt and pepper to taste. Sprinkle the flour on both sides of the pork chops, then coat both sides with the bread crumbs and Parmesan cheese.
2. **Air Frying.** Place the pork chops in the Chefman air fryer. Stacking them is okay. Spray the pork chops with cooking oil. Cook for 6 minutes.
   Open the Chefman air fryer and flip the pork chops. Cook for an additional 6 minutes.
   Cool before serving. Instead of seasoning salt, you can use either chicken or pork rub for additional flavor. You can find these rubs in the spice aisle of the grocery store.

PER SERVING: CALORIES: 334; FAT: 7G; PROTEIN:34G; FIBER:0G

Crispy Roast Garlic-Salt Pork

PREP: 5 MINUTES • COOK TIME: 45 MINUTES • TOTAL: 50 MINUTES
SERVES: 4

Ingredients
1 teaspoon Chinese five spice powder
1 teaspoon white pepper
2 pounds pork belly
2 teaspoons garlic salt

Directions:
1 **Preparing the Ingredients.** Preheat the air fryer to 390°F.
 Mix all the spices in a bowl to create the dry rub.
 Score the skin of the pork belly with a knife and season the entire pork with the spice rub.
2 **Air Frying.** Place in the air fryer basket and cook for 40 to 45 minutes until the skin is crispy.
 Chop before serving.

PER SERVING: CALORIES: 785; FAT:80.7G; PROTEIN:14.2G; FIBER:0G

Peanut Satay Pork

PREP: 5 MINUTES • COOK TIME: 12 MINUTES • TOTAL: 17 MINUTES
SERVES: 5

Ingredients
11 Ozs Pork Fillet, sliced into bite sized strips
4 Cloves Garlic, crushed
1 Tsp Ginger Powder
2 Tsps Chili Paste
2 Tbsps Sweet Soy Sauce (Kecap Manis)
2 Tbsps Vegetable Oil
1 Shallot, finely chopped
1 Tsp Ground Coriander
3/4 Cup Coconut Milk
1/3 Cup Peanuts, ground

Directions:
1 **Preparing the Ingredients.** Mix half of the garlic in a dish with the ginger, a tablespoon of sweet soy sauce, and a tablespoon of the oil. Combine the meat into the mixture and leave to marinate for 15 minutes
 Preheat the Chefman air fryer to 390 degrees
2 **Air Frying.** Place the marinated meat into the Chefman air fryer. Set the timer to 12 minutes and roast the meat until brown and done. Turn once while roasting
 In the meantime, make the peanut sauce by heating the remaining tablespoon of oil in a saucepan and gently sauté the shallot with the garlic. Add the coriander and fry until fragrant
 Mix the coconut milk and the peanuts with the chili paste and remaining soy sauce with the shallot mixture and gently boil for 5 minutes, while stirring
 Drizzle over the cooked meat and serve with rice

Crispy Breaded Pork Chops

PREP: 10 MINUTES • COOK TIME: 15 MINUTES • TOTAL: 25 MINUTES
SERVES: 8

Ingredients
1/8 tsp. pepper
¼ tsp. chili powder
½ tsp. onion powder
½ tsp. garlic powder
1 ¼ tsp. sweet paprika
2 tbsp. grated parmesan cheese
1/3 C. crushed cornflake crumbs
½ C. panko breadcrumbs
1 beaten egg
6 center-cut boneless pork chops

Directions:

1 **Preparing the Ingredients.** Ensure that your air fryer is preheated to 400 degrees. Spray the basket with olive oil.
   With ½ teaspoon salt and pepper, season both sides of pork chops.
   Combine ¾ teaspoon salt with pepper, chili powder, onion powder, garlic powder, paprika, cornflake crumbs, panko breadcrumbs and parmesan cheese.
   Beat egg in another bowl.
   Dip pork chops into the egg and then crumb mixture.
   Add pork chops to air fryer and spritz with olive oil.
2 **Air Frying.** Set temperature to 400°F, and set time to 12 minutes. Cook 12 minutes, making sure to flip over halfway through cooking process.
   Only add 3 chops in at a time and repeat the process with remaining pork chops.

PER SERVING: CALORIES: 378; FAT: 13G; PROTEIN:33G; SUGAR:1G

Ginger, Garlic And Pork Dumplings

PREP: 10 MINUTES • COOK TIME: 15 MINUTES • TOTAL: 25 MINUTES
SERVES: 8

Ingredients
¼ teaspoon crushed red pepper
½ teaspoon sugar
1 tablespoon chopped fresh ginger
1 tablespoon chopped garlic
1 teaspoon canola oil
1 teaspoon toasted sesame oil
18 dumpling wrappers
2 tablespoons rice vinegar
2 teaspoons soy sauce
4 cups bok choy, chopped
4 ounces ground pork

Directions:

1 **Preparing the Ingredients.** Heat oil in a skillet and sauté the ginger and garlic until fragrant. Stir in the ground pork and cook for 5 minutes.
   Stir in the bok choy and crushed red pepper. Season with salt and pepper to taste. Allow to cool.
   Place the meat mixture in the middle of the dumpling wrappers. Fold the wrappers to seal the meat mixture in.
   Place the bok choy in the grill pan.
2 **Air Frying.** Cook the dumplings in the air fryer at 330°F for 15 minutes.
   Meanwhile, prepare the dipping sauce by combining the remaining Ingredients in a bowl.

PER SERVING: CALORIES: 137; FAT: 5G; PROTEIN:7G

Caramelized Pork Shoulder

PREP: 10 MINUTES • COOK TIME: 20 MINUTES • TOTAL: 30 MINUTES
SERVES: 8

Ingredients

1/3 cup soy sauce
2 tablespoons sugar
1 tablespoon honey
2 pound pork shoulder, cut into 1½-inch thick slices

Directions:

1 **Preparing the Ingredients**. In a bowl, mix together all ingredients except pork. Add pork and coat with marinade generously.
    Cover and refrigerate o marinate for about 2-8 hours.
    Preheat the Chefman air fryer to 335 degrees F.
2 **Air Frying.** Place the pork in an Air fryer basket.
    Cook for about 10 minutes.
    Now, set the Chefman air fryer to 390 degrees F. Cook for about 10 minutes

Curry Pork Roast in Coconut Sauce

PREP: 10 MINUTES • COOK TIME: 60 MINUTES • TOTAL: 70 MINUTES
SERVES: 6

Ingredients

½ teaspoon curry powder
½ teaspoon ground turmeric powder
1 can unsweetened coconut milk
1 tablespoons sugar
2 tablespoons fish sauce
2 tablespoons soy sauce
3 pounds pork shoulder
Salt and pepper to taste

Directions:

1 **Preparing the Ingredients.** Place all Ingredients in bowl and allow the meat to marinate in the fridge for at least 2 hours.
    Preheat the air fryer to 390°F.
    Place the grill pan accessory in the air fryer.
2 **Air Frying.** Grill the meat for 20 minutes making sure to flip the pork every 10 minutes for even grilling and cook in batches.
    Meanwhile, pour the marinade in a saucepan and allow to simmer for 10 minutes until the sauce thickens.
    Baste the pork with the sauce before serving.

PER SERVING: CALORIES: 688; FAT: 52G; PROTEIN:17G

Chinese Salt and Pepper Pork Chop Stir-fry

PREP: 10 MINUTES • COOK TIME: 15 MINUTES • TOTAL: 25 MINUTES

SERVES: 4

Ingredients

Pork Chops:

Olive oil

¾ C. almond flour

¼ tsp. pepper

½ tsp. salt

1 egg white

Pork Chops

Stir-fry:

¼ tsp. pepper

1 tsp. sea salt

2 tbsp. olive oil

2 sliced scallions

2 sliced jalapeno peppers

Directions:

1 **Preparing the Ingredients.** Coat the Chefman air fryer basket with olive oil. Whisk pepper, salt, and egg white together till foamy.

   Cut pork chops into pieces, leaving just a bit on bones. Pat dry.

   Add pieces of pork to egg white mixture, coating well. Let sit for marinade 20 minutes.

   Put marinated chops into a large bowl and add almond flour. Dredge and shake off excess and place into air fryer.

2 **Air Frying**. Set temperature to 360°F, and set time to 12 minutes. Cook 12 minutes at 360 degrees.

   Turn up the heat to 400 degrees and cook another 6 minutes till pork chops are nice and crisp.

   To make stir-fry, remove jalapeno seeds and chop up. Chop scallions and mix with jalapeno pieces.

Heat a skillet with olive oil. Stir-fry pepper, salt, scallions, and jalapenos 60 seconds. Then add fried pork pieces to skills and toss with scallion mixture. Stir-fry 1-2 minutes till well coated and hot.

PER SERVING: CALORIES: 294; FAT: 17G; PROTEIN:36G; SUGAR:4G

Roasted Pork Tenderloin

PREP: 5 MINUTES • COOK TIME: 1 HOUR • TOTAL: 65 MINUTES
SERVES: 4

Ingredients

1 (3-pound) pork tenderloin
2 tablespoons extra-virgin olive oil
2 garlic cloves, minced
1 teaspoon dried basil
1 teaspoon dried oregano
1 teaspoon dried thyme
Salt
Pepper

Directions:

1 **Preparing the Ingredients.** Drizzle the pork tenderloin with the olive oil.
Rub the garlic, basil, oregano, thyme, and salt and pepper to taste all over the tenderloin.
2 **Air Frying.** Place the tenderloin in the Chefman air fryer. Cook for 45 minutes. Use a meat thermometer to test for doneness
Open the Chefman air fryer and flip the pork tenderloin. Cook for an additional 15 minutes.
Remove the cooked pork from the air fryer and allow it to rest for 10 minutes before cutting.

PER SERVING: CALORIES: 283; FAT: 10G; PROTEIN:48G

Garlic Putter Pork Chops

PREP: 10 MINUTES • COOK TIME: 7 MINUTES • TOTAL: 17 MINUTES
SERVES: 4

Ingredients

2 tsp. parsley
2 tsp. grated garlic cloves
1 tbsp. coconut oil
1 tbsp. coconut butter
4 pork chops

Directions:

1 **Preparing the Ingredients.** Ensure your air fryer is preheated to 350 degrees.
Mix butter, coconut oil, and all seasoning together. Then rub seasoning mixture over all sides of pork chops. Place in foil, seal, and chill for 1 hour.
Remove pork chops from foil and place into air fryer.
2 **Air Frying.** Set temperature to 350°F, and set time to 7 minutes. Cook 7 minutes on one side and 8 minutes on the other.
Drizzle with olive oil and serve alongside a green salad.

PER SERVING: CALORIES: 526; FAT: 23G; PROTEIN:41G; SUGAR:4G

Fried Pork with Sweet and Sour Glaze

PREP: 5 MINUTES • COOK TIME: 30 MINUTES • TOTAL: 35 MINUTES
SERVES: 4

Ingredients

¼ cup rice wine vinegar
¼ teaspoon Chinese five spice powder
1 cup potato starch
1 green onion, chopped
2 large eggs, beaten
2 pounds pork chops cut into chunks
2 tablespoons cornstarch + 3 tablespoons water
5 tablespoons brown sugar
Salt and pepper to taste

Directions:

1 **Preparing the Ingredients.** Preheat the air fryer to 390°F.
  Season pork chops with salt and pepper to taste.
  Dip the pork chops in egg. Set aside.
  In a bowl, combine the potato starch and Chinese five spice powder.
  Dredge the pork chops in the flour mixture.
2 **Air Frying.** Place in the double layer rack and cook for 30 minutes.
  Meanwhile, place the vinegar and brown sugar in a saucepan. Season with salt and pepper to taste. Stir in the cornstarch slurry and allow to simmer until thick.
  Serve the pork chops with the sauce and garnish with green onions.

PER SERVING: CALORIES: 420; FAT: 11.8G; PROTEIN:69.2G

Pork Cutlet Rolls

PREP: 10 MINUTES • COOK TIME: 15 MINUTES • TOTAL: 25 MINUTES
SERVES: 4

Ingredients

4 Pork Cutlets
4 Sundried Tomatoes in oil
2 Tbsps Parsley, finely chopped
1 Green Onion, finely chopped
Black Pepper to taste
2 Tsps Paprika
1/2 Tbsp Olive Oil
* String for Rolled Meat

Directions:

1 **Preparing the Ingredients.** Preheat the Chefman air fryer to 390 degrees
  Finely chop the tomatoes and mix with the parsley and green onion. Add salt and pepper to taste
  Spread out the cutlets and coat them with the tomato mixture. Roll up the cutlets and secure intact with the string
  Rub the rolls with salt, pepper, and paprika powder and thinly coat them with olive oil
2 **Air Frying**. Put the cutlet rolls in the Chefman air fryer tray and cook for 15 minutes. Roast until nicely brown and done.
  Serve with tomato sauce.

Oregano-Paprika on Breaded Pork

PREP: 10 MINUTES • COOK TIME: 30 MINUTES • TOTAL: 40 MINUTES

SERVES: 4

Ingredients

¼ cup water
¼ teaspoon dry mustard
½ teaspoon black pepper
½ teaspoon cayenne pepper
½ teaspoon garlic powder
½ teaspoon salt
1 cup panko breadcrumbs
1 egg, beaten
2 teaspoons oregano
4 lean pork chops
4 teaspoons paprika

Directions:

1 **Preparing the Ingredients.** Preheat the Chefman air fryer to 390°F.
   Pat dry the pork chops.
   In a mixing bowl, combine the egg and water. Then set aside.
   In another bowl, combine the rest of the Ingredients.
   Dip the pork chops in the egg mixture and dredge in the flour mixture.
2 **Air Frying.** Place in the air fryer basket and cook for 25 to 30 minutes until golden.

PER SERVING: CALORIES: 364; FAT: 20.2G; PROTEIN:42.9G

Bacon Wrapped Pork Tenderloin

PREP: 5 MINUTES • COOK TIME: 15 MINUTES • TOTAL: 20 MINUTES

SERVES: 4

Ingredients

Pork:
1-2 tbsp. Dijon mustard
3-4 strips of bacon
1 pork tenderloin
Apple Gravy:
½ - 1 tsp. Dijon mustard
1 tbsp. almond flour
2 tbsp. ghee
1 chopped onion
2-3 Granny Smith apples
1 C. vegetable broth

Directions:

1 **Preparing the Ingredients.** Spread Dijon mustard all over tenderloin and wrap meat with strips of bacon.
2 **Air Frying.** Place into the Chefman air fryer, set temperature to 360°F, and set time to 15 minutes and cook 10-15 minutes at 360 degrees. Use a meat thermometer to check for doneness.
   To make sauce, heat ghee in a pan and add shallots. Cook 1-2 minutes.
   Then add apples, cooking 3-5 minutes until softened.
   Add flour and ghee to make a roux. Add broth and mustard, stirring well to combine.
   When sauce starts to bubble, add 1 cup of sautéed apples, cooking till sauce thickens.
   Once pork tenderloin I cook, allow to sit 5-10 minutes to rest before slicing.
   Serve topped with apple gravy. Devour!

PER SERVING: CALORIES: 552; FAT: 25G; PROTEIN:29G; SUGAR:6G

Pork Tenders With Bell Peppers

PREP: 5 MINUTES • COOK TIME: 15 MINUTES • TOTAL: 20 MINUTES
SERVES: 4

Ingredients

11 Ozs Pork Tenderloin
1 Bell Pepper, in thin strips
1 Red Onion, sliced
2 Tsps Provencal Herbs
Black Pepper to taste
1 Tbsp Olive Oil
1/2 Tbsp Mustard
* Round Oven Dish

Directions:

1 **Preparing the Ingredients.** Preheat the Chefman air fryer to 390 degrees. In the oven dish, mix the bell pepper strips with the onion, herbs, and some salt and pepper to taste. Add half a tablespoon of olive oil to the mixture Cut the pork tenderloin into four pieces and rub with salt, pepper and mustard. Thinly coat the pieces with remaining olive oil and place them upright in the oven dish on top of the pepper mixture

2 **Air Frying.** Place the bowl into the Chefman air fryer. Set the timer to 15 minutes and roast the meat and the vegetables
Turn the meat and mix the peppers halfway through.
Serve with a fresh salad.

Dijon Garlic Pork Tenderloin

PREP: 5 MINUTES • COOK TIME: 10 MINUTES • TOTAL: 15 MINUTES
SERVES: 6

Ingredients

1 C. breadcrumbs
Pinch of cayenne pepper
3 crushed garlic cloves
2 tbsp. ground ginger
2 tbsp. Dijon mustard
2 tbsp. raw honey
4 tbsp. water
2 tsp. salt
1 pound pork tenderloin, sliced into 1-inch rounds

Directions:

1 **Preparing the Ingredients.** With pepper and salt, season all sides of tenderloin. Combine cayenne pepper, garlic, ginger, mustard, honey, and water until smooth. Dip pork rounds into honey mixture and then into breadcrumbs, ensuring they all get coated well.
Place coated pork rounds into your Chefman air fryer.

2 **Air Frying.** Set temperature to 400°F, and set time to 10 minutes. Cook 10 minutes at 400 degrees. Flip and then cook an additional 5 minutes until golden in color.

PER SERVING: CALORIES: 423; FAT: 18G; PROTEIN:31G; SUGAR:3G

Pork Neck with Salad

PREP: 10 MINUTES • COOK TIME: 12 MINUTES • TOTAL: 22 MINUTES
SERVES: 2

Ingredients

For Pork:
1 tablespoon soy sauce
1 tablespoon fish sauce
½ tablespoon oyster sauce
½ pound pork neck
For Salad:
1 ripe tomato, sliced tickly
8-10 Thai shallots, sliced
1 scallion, chopped
1 bunch fresh basil leaves
1 bunch fresh cilantro leaves
For Dressing:
3 tablespoons fish sauce
2 tablespoons olive oil
1 teaspoon apple cider vinegar
1 tablespoon palm sugar
2 bird eye chili
1 tablespoon garlic, minced

Directions:

1 **Preparing the Ingredients.** For pork in a bowl, mix together all ingredients except pork.
Add pork neck and coat with marinade evenly. Refrigerate for about 2-3 hours.
Preheat the Chefman air fryer to 340 degrees F.
2 **Air Frying**. Place the pork neck onto a grill pan. Cook for about 12 minutes.
Meanwhile in a large salad bowl, mix together all salad ingredients.
In a bowl, add all dressing ingredients and beat till well combined.
Remove pork neck from Air fryer and cut into desired slices.
Place pork slices over salad.

Cajun Pork Steaks

PREP: 5 MINUTES • COOK TIME: 20 MINUTES • TOTAL: 25 MINUTES
SERVES: 6

Ingredients

4-6 pork steaks
BBQ sauce:
Cajun seasoning
1 tbsp. vinegar
1 tsp. low-sodium soy sauce
½ C. brown sugar
½ C. vegan ketchup

Directions:

1 **Preparing the Ingredients.** Ensure your air fryer is preheated to 290 degrees. Sprinkle pork steaks with Cajun seasoning.
Combine remaining ingredients and brush onto steaks. Add coated steaks to air fryer.
2 **Air Frying**. Set temperature to 290°F, and set time to 20 minutes. Cook 15-20 minutes till just browned.

PER SERVING: CALORIES: 209; FAT: 11G; PROTEIN:28G; SUGAR:2G

Wonton Taco Cups

PREP: 5 MINUTES • COOK TIME: 10 MINUTES • TOTAL: 15 MINUTES
SERVES: 8

Ingredients

1/2 pound ground pork, browned and drained
1/2 pound ground beef, browned and drained
1 envelope taco seasoning
1 (10-ounce) can tomatoes with chilies, diced and drained
1 bell pepper, seeded and chopped
32 wonton wrappers
1 cup Cheddar cheese, shredded

Directions:

1 **Preparing the Ingredients.** Combine the pork, beef, taco seasoning, diced tomatoes, and bell pepper; mix well.
Line all the muffin cups with wonton wrappers. Spritz with a nonstick cooking oil. Divide the beef filling among wrappers; top with the shredded cheese.
2 **Air Frying.** Bake at 370 degrees F for about 10 minutes or until heated through.

Cajun Sweet-Sour Grilled Pork

PREP: 5 MINUTES • COOK TIME: 12 MINUTES • TOTAL: 17 MINUTES
SERVES: 3

Ingredients

¼ cup brown sugar
1/4 cup cider vinegar
1-lb pork loin, sliced into 1-inch cubes
2 tablespoons Cajun seasoning
3 tablespoons brown sugar

Directions:

1 **Preparing the Ingredients.** In a shallow dish, mix well pork loin, 3 tablespoons brown sugar, and Cajun seasoning. Toss well to coat. Marinate in the ref for 3 hours. In a medium bowl mix well, brown sugar and vinegar for basting.
Thread pork pieces in skewers. Baste with sauce and place on skewer rack in air fryer.
2 **Air Frying.** For 12 minutes, cook on 360°F. Halfway through cooking time, turnover skewers and baste with sauce. If needed, cook in batches.
Serve and enjoy.

PER SERVING: CALORIES: 428; FAT: 16.7G; PROTEIN:39G; SUGAR:2G

Chinese Braised Pork Belly

PREP: 5 MINUTES • COOK TIME: 20 MINUTES • TOTAL: 25 MINUTES
SERVES: 8

Ingredients
1 lb Pork Belly, sliced
1 Tbsp Oyster Sauce
1 Tbsp Sugar
2 Red Fermented Bean Curds
1 Tbsp Red Fermented Bean Curd Paste
1 Tbsp Cooking Wine
1/2 Tbsp Soy Sauce
1 Tsp Sesame Oil
1 Cup All Purpose Flour

Directions:
1 **Preparing the Ingredients.** Preheat the Chefman air fryer to 390 degrees.
In a small bowl, mix all ingredients together and rub the pork thoroughly with this mixture
Set aside to marinate for at least 30 minutes or preferably overnight for the flavors to permeate the meat
Coat each marinated pork belly slice in flour and place in the Chefman air fryer tray
2 **Air Frying.** Cook for 15 to 20 minutes until crispy and tender.

Air Fryer Sweet and Sour Pork

PREP: 10 MINUTES • COOK TIME: 12 MINUTES • TOTAL: 22 MINUTES
SERVES: 6

Ingredients
3 tbsp. olive oil
1/16 tsp. Chinese Five Spice
¼ tsp. pepper
½ tsp. sea salt
1 tsp. pure sesame oil
2 eggs
1 C. almond flour
2 pounds pork, sliced into chunks
  Sweet and Sour Sauce:
¼ tsp. sea salt
½ tsp. garlic powder
1 tbsp. low-sodium soy sauce
½ C. rice vinegar
5 tbsp. tomato paste
1/8 tsp. water
½ C. sweetener of choice

Directions:
1 **Preparing the Ingredients.** To make the dipping sauce, whisk all sauce ingredients together over medium heat, stirring 5 minutes. Simmer uncovered 5 minutes till thickened.
Meanwhile, combine almond flour, five spice, pepper, and salt.
In another bowl, mix eggs with sesame oil. Dredge pork in flour mixture and then in egg mixture. Shake any excess off before adding to air fryer basket.
2 **Air Frying**. Set temperature to 340°F, and set time to 12 minutes.
Serve with sweet and sour dipping sauce!

PER SERVING: CALORIES: 371; FAT: 17G; PROTEIN:27G; SUGAR:1G

Pork Loin with Potatoes

PREP: 10 MINUTES • COOK TIME: 25 MINUTES • TOTAL: 35 MINUTES SERVES: 2

Ingredients

2 pounds pork loin
1 teaspoon fresh parsley, chopped
2 large red potatoes, chopped
½ teaspoon garlic powder
½ teaspoon red pepper flakes, crushed
Salt and freshly ground black pepper, to taste

Directions:

1 **Preparing the Ingredients.** In a large bowl, add all ingredients except glaze and toss to coat well. Preheat the Air fryer to 325 degrees F. Place the loin in the Chefman air fryer basket.
Arrange the potatoes around pork loin.
2 **Air Frying.** Cook for about 25 minutes.

Fried Pork Scotch Egg

PREP: 10 MINUTES • COOK TIME: 25 MINUTES • TOTAL: 35 MINUTES SERVES: 2

Ingredients

3 soft-boiled eggs, peeled
8 ounces of raw minced pork, or sausage outside the casings
2 teaspoons of ground rosemary
2 teaspoons of garlic powder
Pinch of salt and pepper
2 raw eggs
1 cup of breadcrumbs (Panko, but other brands are fine, or home-made bread crumbs work too)

Directions:

1. **Preparing the Ingredients.** Cover the basket of the Chefman air fryer with a lining of tin foil, leaving the edges uncovered to allow air to circulate through the basket. Preheat the air fryer to 350 degrees.
In a mixing bowl, combine the raw pork with the rosemary, garlic powder, salt and pepper. This will probably be easiest to do with your masher or bare hands (though make sure to wash thoroughly after handling raw meat!); combine until all the spices are evenly spread throughout the meat.
Divide the meat mixture into three equal portions in the mixing bowl, and form each into balls with your hands.
Lay a large sheet of plastic wrap on the countertop, and flatten one of the balls of meat on top of it, to form a wide, flat meat-circle.
Place one of the peeled soft-boiled eggs in the center of the meat-circle and then, using the ends of the plastic wrap, pull the

meat-circle so that it is fully covering and surrounding the soft-boiled egg.

Tighten and shape the plastic wrap covering the meat so that if forms a ball, and make sure not to squeeze too hard lest you squish the soft-boiled egg at the center of the ball! Set aside.

Repeat steps 5-7 with the other two soft-boiled eggs and portions of meat-mixture.

In a separate mixing bowl, beat the two raw eggs until fluffy and until the yolks and whites are fully combined.

One by one, remove the plastic wrap and dunk the pork-covered balls into the raw egg, and then roll them in the bread crumbs, covering fully and generously.

Place each of the bread-crumb covered meat-wrapped balls onto the foil-lined surface of the air fryer. Three of them should fit nicely, without touching.

2. **Air Frying.** Set the Chefman air fryer timer to 25 minutes.

About halfway through the cooking time, shake the handle of the air-fryer vigorously, so that the scotch eggs inside roll around and ensure full coverage.

After 25 minutes, the air fryer will shut off and the scotch eggs should be perfect – the meat fully cooked, the egg-yolks still runny on the inside, and the outsides crispy and golden-brown. Using tongs, place them on serving plates, slice in half, and enjoy

Roasted Char Siew (Pork Butt)

PREP: 10 MINUTES • COOK TIME: 25 MINUTES • TOTAL: 35 MINUTES
SERVES: 6

Ingredients
1 strip of pork shoulder butt with a good amount of fat marbling
Marinade:
1 tsp. sesame oil
4 tbsp. raw honey
1 tsp. low-sodium dark soy sauce
1 tsp. light soy sauce
1 tbsp. rose wine
2 tbsp. Hoisin sauce

Directions:

1 **Preparing the Ingredients.** Combine all marinade ingredients together and add to Ziploc bag. Place pork in bag, making sure all sections of pork strip are engulfed in the marinade. Chill 3-24 hours.

   Take out the strip 30 minutes before planning to cook and preheat your air fryer to 350 degrees.

   Place foil on small pan and brush with olive oil. Place marinated pork strip onto prepared pan.

2 **Air Frying**. Set temperature to 350°F, and set time to 20 minutes. Roast 20 minutes. Glaze with marinade every 5-10 minutes. Remove strip and leave to cool a few minutes before slicing.

PER SERVING: CALORIES: 289; FAT: 13G; PROTEIN:33G; SUGAR:1G

Juicy Pork Ribs Ole

PREP: 10 MINUTES • COOK TIME: 25 MINUTES • TOTAL: 35 MINUTES
SERVES: 4

Ingredients
1 rack of pork ribs
1/2 cup low-fat milk
1 tablespoon envelope taco seasoning mix
1 can tomato sauce
1/2 teaspoon ground black pepper
1 teaspoon seasoned salt
1 tablespoon cornstarch
1 teaspoon canola oil

Directions:
1. **Preparing the Ingredients.** Place all ingredients in a mixing dish; let them marinate for 1 hour.
2. **Air Frying.** Cook the marinated ribs approximately 25 minutes at 390 degrees F

Work with batches. Enjoy

Asian Pork Chops

PREP: 2 HOURS 10 MINUTES • COOK TIME: 15 MINUTES • TOTAL:2 HOURS, 25 MINUTES
SERVES: 4

Ingredients
1/2 cup hoisin sauce
3 tablespoons cider vinegar
1 tablespoon Asian sweet chili sauce
1/4 teaspoon garlic powder
4 (1/2-inch-thick) boneless pork chops
1 teaspoon salt
1/2 teaspoon pepper

Directions:
1. **Preparing the Ingredients.** Stir together hoisin, chili sauce, garlic powder, and vinegar in a large mixing bowl. Separate 1/4 cup of this mixture, then add pork chops to the bowl and marinate in the fridge for 2 hours. Remove the pork chops and place them on a plate. Sprinkle each side of the pork chop evenly with salt and pepper.
2. **Air Frying.** Cook at 360 degrees for 14 minutes, flipping half way through. Brush with reserved marinade and serve.

PER SERVING: CALORIES: 338; FAT: 21G; PROTEIN:19G; FIBER:1G

Teriyaki Pork Rolls

PREP: 10 MINUTES • COOK TIME: 8 MINUTES • TOTAL: 20 MINUTES SERVES: 6

Ingredients

1 tsp. almond flour
4 tbsp. low-sodium soy sauce
4 tbsp. mirin
4 tbsp. brown sugar
Thumb-sized amount of ginger, chopped
Pork belly slices
Enoki mushrooms

Directions:

1 **Preparing the Ingredients.** Mix brown sugar, mirin, soy sauce, almond flour, and ginger together until brown sugar dissolves.
   Take pork belly slices and wrap around a bundle of mushrooms. Brush each roll with teriyaki sauce. Chill half an hour. Preheat your Chefman air fryer to 350 degrees and add marinated pork rolls.
2 **Air Frying.** Set temperature to 350°F, and set time to 8 minutes.

PER SERVING: CALORIES: 412; FAT: 9G; PROTEIN:19G; SUGAR:4G

Ham and Cheese Rollups

PREP: 5 MINUTES • COOK TIME: 8 MINUTES • TOTAL: 15 MINUTES SERVES: 12

Ingredients

2 tsp. raw honey
2 tsp. dried parsley
1 tbsp. poppy seeds
½ C. melted coconut oil
¼ C. spicy brown mustard
9 slices of provolone cheese
10 ounces of thinly sliced Black Forest Ham
1 tube of crescent rolls

Directions:

1 **Preparing the Ingredients.** Roll out dough into a rectangle. Spread 2-3 tablespoons of spicy mustard onto dough, then layer provolone cheese and ham slices.
   Roll the filled dough up as tight as you can and slice into 12-15 pieces.
   Melt coconut oil and mix with a pinch of salt and pepper, parsley, honey, and remaining mustard.
   Brush mustard mixture over roll-ups and sprinkle with poppy seeds.
   Grease air fryer basket liberally with olive oil and add rollups.
2 **Air Frying.** Set temperature to 350°F, and set time to 8 minutes.
   Serve!

PER SERVING: CALORIES: 289; FAT: 6G; PROTEIN:18G; SUGAR

Vietnamese Pork Chops

PREP: 10 MINUTES • COOK TIME: 7 MINUTES • TOTAL: 25 MINUTES
SERVES: 6

Ingredients

1 tbsp. olive oil
1 tbsp. fish sauce
1 tsp. low-sodium dark soy sauce
1 tsp. pepper
3 tbsp. lemongrass
1 tbsp. chopped shallot
1 tbsp. chopped garlic
1 tbsp. brown sugar
2 pork chops

Directions:

1   **Preparing the Ingredients.** Add pork chops to a bowl along with olive oil, fish sauce, soy sauce, pepper, lemongrass, shallot, garlic, and brown sugar.
    Marinade pork chops 2 hours.
    Ensure your air fryer is preheated to 400 degrees. Add pork chops to the basket.
2   **Air Frying**. Set temperature to 400°F, and set time to 7 minutes. Cook making sure to flip after 5 minutes of cooking.
    Serve alongside steamed cauliflower rice.

PER SERVING: CALORIES: 290; FAT: 15G; PROTEIN:30G; SUGAR:3G

Cheeseburger Egg Rolls

PREP: 10 MINUTES • COOK TIME: 7 MINUTES • TOTAL: 17 MINUTES
SERVES: 6

Ingredients

6 egg roll wrappers
6 chopped dill pickle chips
1 tbsp. yellow mustard
3 tbsp. cream cheese
3 tbsp. shredded cheddar cheese
½ C. chopped onion
½ C. chopped bell pepper
¼ tsp. onion powder
¼ tsp. garlic powder
8 ounces of raw lean ground beef

Directions:

1 **Preparing the Ingredients.** In a skillet, add seasonings, beef, onion, and bell pepper. Stir and crumble beef till fully cooked, and vegetables are soft.
Take skillet off the heat and add cream cheese, mustard, and cheddar cheese, stirring till melted.
Pour beef mixture into a bowl and fold in pickles.
Lay out egg wrappers and place 1/6th of beef mixture into each one. Moisten egg roll wrapper edges with water. Fold sides to the middle and seal with water.
Repeat with all other egg rolls.
Place rolls into air fryer, one batch at a time.
2 **Air Frying.** Set temperature to 392°F, and set time to 7 minutes.

PER SERVING: CALORIES: 153; FAT: 4G; PROTEIN:12G; SUGAR:3G

Air Fried Grilled Steak

PREP: 5 MINUTES • COOK TIME: 45 MINUTES • TOTAL: 50 MINUTES
SERVES: 2

Ingredients

2 top sirloin steaks
3 tablespoons butter, melted
3 tablespoons olive oil
Salt and pepper to taste

Directions:

1 **Preparing the Ingredients.** Preheat the Chefman air fryer for 5 minutes.
Season the sirloin steaks with olive oil, salt and pepper.
Place the beef in the air fryer basket.
2 **Air Frying.** Cook for 45 minutes at 350°F. Once cooked, serve with butter.

ER SERVING: CALORIES: 1536; FAT: 123.7G; PROTEIN:103.4G

Juicy Cheeseburgers

PREP: 5 MINUTES • COOK TIME: 15 MINUTES • TOTAL: 20 MINUTES
SERVES: 4

Ingredients

1 pound 93% lean ground beef
1 teaspoon Worcestershire sauce
1 tablespoon burger seasoning
Salt
Pepper
Cooking oil
4 slices cheese
3 buns

Directions:

1 **Preparing the Ingredients.** In a large bowl, mix the ground beef, Worcestershire, burger seasoning, and salt and pepper to taste until well blended. Spray the air fryer basket with cooking oil. You will need only a quick spritz. The burgers will produce oil as they cook. Shape the mixture into 4 patties. Place the burgers in the air fryer. The burgers should fit without the need to stack, but stacking is okay if necessary.

2 **Air Frying.** Cook for 8 minutes. Open the air fryer and flip the burgers. Cook for an additional 3 to 4 minutes. Check the inside of the burgers to determine if they have finished cooking. You can stick a knife or fork in the center to examine the color.
Top each burger with a slice of cheese. Cook for an additional minute, or until the cheese has melted. Serve on buns with any additional toppings of your choice.

PER SERVING: CALORIES: 566; FAT: 39G; PROTEIN:29G; FIBER:1G

Spicy Thai Beef Stir-Fry

PREP: 15 MINUTES • COOK TIME: 9 MINUTES • TOTAL: 24 MINUTES
SERVES: 4

Ingredients

1 pound sirloin steaks, thinly sliced
2 tablespoons lime juice, divided
⅓ cup crunchy peanut butter
½ cup beef broth
1 tablespoon olive oil
1½ cups broccoli florets
2 cloves garlic, sliced
1 to 2 red chile peppers, sliced

Directions:

1 **Preparing the Ingredients.** In a medium bowl, combine the steak with 1 tablespoon of the lime juice. Set aside.
Combine the peanut butter and beef broth in a small bowl and mix well. Drain the beef and add the juice from the bowl into the peanut butter mixture.
In a 6-inch metal bowl, combine the olive oil, steak, and broccoli.

2 **Air Frying.** Cook for 3 to 4 minutes or until the steak is almost cooked and the broccoli is crisp and tender, shaking the basket once during cooking time.
Add the garlic, chile peppers, and the peanut butter mixture and stir.
Cook for 3 to 5 minutes or until the sauce is bubbling and the broccoli is tender.
Serve over hot rice.

PER SERVING: CALORIES: 387; FAT: 22G; PROTEIN:42G; FIBER:2G

Beef Brisket Recipe from Texas

PREP: 15 MINUTES • COOK TIME: 1HOUR AND 30 MINUTES MINUTES
SERVES: 8

Ingredients
1 ½ cup beef stock
1 bay leaf
1 tablespoon garlic powder
1 tablespoon onion powder
2 pounds beef brisket, trimmed
2 tablespoons chili powder
2 teaspoons dry mustard
4 tablespoons olive oil
Salt and pepper to taste

Directions:
1 **Preparing the Ingredients.** Preheat the Chefman air fryer for 5 minutes. Place all ingredients in a deep baking dish that will fit in the air fryer.
2 **Air Frying.** Bake for 1 hour and 30 minutes at 400°F.
   Stir the beef every after 30 minutes to soak in the sauce.

PER SERVING: CALORIES: 306; FAT: 24.1G; PROTEIN:18.3G

Copycat Taco Bell Crunch Wraps

PREP: 10 MINUTES • COOK TIME: 2 MINUTES • TOTAL: 15 MINUTES
SERVES: 6

Ingredients
6 wheat tostadas
2 C. sour cream
2 C. Mexican blend cheese
2 C. shredded lettuce
12 ounces low-sodium nacho cheese
3 Roma tomatoes
6 12-inch wheat tortillas
1 1/3 C. water
2 packets low-sodium taco seasoning
2 pounds of lean ground beef

Directions:
1 **Preparing the Ingredients.** Ensure your Chefman air fryer is preheated to 400 degrees.
   Make beef according to taco seasoning packets.
   Place 2/3 C. prepared beef, 4 tbsp. cheese, 1 tostada, 1/3 C. sour cream, 1/3 C. lettuce, 1/6th of tomatoes and 1/3 C. cheese on each tortilla.
   Fold up tortillas edges and repeat with remaining ingredients.
   Lay the folded sides of tortillas down into the air fryer and spray with olive oil.
2 **Air Frying.** Set temperature to 400°F, and set time to 2 minutes. Cook 2 minutes till browned.

PER SERVING: CALORIES: 311; FAT: 9G; PROTEIN:22G; SUGAR:2G

Steak and Mushroom Gravy

PREP: 15 MINUTES • COOK TIME: 15 MINUTES • TOTAL: 30 MINUTES
SERVES: 4

Ingredients

4 cubed steaks
2 large eggs
1/2 dozen mushrooms
4 tablespoons unsalted butter
4 tablespoons black pepper
2 tablespoons salt
1/2 teaspoon onion powder
1/2 teaspoon garlic powder
1/4 teaspoon cayenne powder
1 1/4 teaspoons paprika
1 1/2 cups whole milk
1/3 cup flour
3   tablespoons vegetable oil

Directions:

1   **Preparing the Ingredients.** Mix 1/2 flour and a pinch of black pepper in a shallow bowl or on a plate.
    Beat 2 eggs in a bowl and mix in a pinch of salt and pepper.
    In another shallow bowl mix together the other half of the flour with a pepper to taste, garlic powder, paprika, cayenne, and onion powder.
    Chop mushrooms and set aside.
    Press your steak into the first flour bowl, then dip in egg, then press the steak into the second flour bowl until covered completely.

2   **Air Frying.** Cook steak in your Chefman air fryer at 360 degrees for 15 Minutes, flipping halfway through.
    While the steak cooks, warm the butter over medium heat and add mushrooms to sauté.

Add 4 tablespoons of the flour and pepper mix to the pan and mix until there are no clumps of flour.
Mix in whole milk and simmer.
Serve over steak for breakfast, lunch, or dinner.

PER SERVING: CALORIES: 442; FAT: 27G; PROTEIN:32G; FIBER:2.3G

Air Fryer Beef Casserole

PREP: 5 MINUTES • COOK TIME: 30 MINUTES • TOTAL: 35 MINUTES
SERVES: 4

Ingredients

1 green bell pepper, seeded and chopped
1 onion, chopped
1-pound ground beef
3 cloves of garlic, minced
3 tablespoons olive oil
6 cups eggs, beaten
Salt and pepper to taste

Directions:

1 **Preparing the Ingredients.** Preheat the air fryer for 5 minutes.
   In a baking dish that will fit in the air fryer, mix the ground beef, onion, garlic, olive oil, and bell pepper. Season with salt and pepper to taste.
   Pour in the beaten eggs and give a good stir.
   Place the dish with the beef and egg mixture in the air fryer.
2 **Air Frying.** Bake for 30 minutes at 325°F.

PER SERVING: CALORIES: 1520; FAT: 125.11G; PROTEIN:87.9G

Meat Lovers' Pizza

PREP: 10 MINUTES • COOK TIME: 12 MINUTES • TOTAL: 22 MINUTES
SERVES: 2

Ingredients

1 pre-prepared 7-inch pizza pie crust, defrosted if necessary.
1/3 cup of marinara sauce.
2 ounces of grilled steak, sliced into bite-sized pieces
2 ounces of salami, sliced fine
2 ounces of pepperoni, sliced fine
¼ cup of American cheese
¼ cup of shredded mozzarella cheese

Directions:

1 **Preparing the Ingredients.** Preheat the Chefman air fryer to 350 degrees. Lay the pizza dough flat on a sheet of parchment paper or tin foil, cut large enough to hold the entire pie crust, but small enough that it will leave the edges of the Chefman air frying basket uncovered to allow for air circulation. Using a fork, stab the pizza dough several times across the surface – piercing the pie crust will allow air to circulate throughout the crust and ensure even cooking. With a deep soup spoon, ladle the marinara sauce onto the pizza dough, and spread evenly in expanding circles over the surface of the pie-crust. Be sure to leave at least ½ inch of bare dough around the edges, to ensure that extra-crispy crunchy first bite of the crust! Distribute the pieces of steak and the slices of salami and pepperoni evenly over the sauce-covered dough, then sprinkle the cheese in an even layer on top.
2 **Air Frying.** Set the Chefman air fryer timer to 12 minutes, and place the pizza with foil or paper on the fryer's basket

surface. Again, be sure to leave the edges of the basket uncovered to allow for proper air circulation, and don't let your bare fingers touch the hot surface. After 12 minutes, when the Chefman air fryer shuts off, the cheese should be perfectly melted and lightly crisped, and the pie crust should be golden brown. Using a spatula – or two, if necessary, remove the pizza from the Chefman air fryer basket and set on a serving plate. Wait a few minutes until the pie is cool enough to handle, then cut into slices and serve.

Chimichurri Skirt Steak

PREP: 10 MINUTES • COOK TIME: 8 MINUTES • TOTAL: 18 MINUTES SERVES: 2

Ingredients

2 x 8 oz Skirt Steak
1 cup Finely Chopped Parsley
¼ cup Finely Chopped Mint
2 Tbsp Fresh Oregano (Washed & finely chopped)
3 Finely Chopped Cloves of Garlic
1 Tsp Red Pepper Flakes (Crushed)
1 Tbsp Ground Cumin
1 Tsp Cayenne Pepper
2 Tsp Smoked Paprika
1 Tsp Salt
¼ Tsp Pepper
¾ cup Oil
3 Tbsp Red Wine Vinegar

Directions:

1 **Preparing the Ingredients.** Throw all the ingredients in a bowl (besides the steak) and mix well.
   Put ¼ cup of the mixture in a plastic baggie with the steak and leave in the fridge overnight (2–24hrs).

2 **Air Frying.** Leave the bag out at room temperature for at least 30 min before popping into the Chefman air fryer. Preheat for a minute or two to 390° F before cooking until med–rare (8–10 min). Put 2 Tbsp of the chimichurri mix on top of each steak before serving.

Country Fried Steak

PREP: 5 MINUTES • COOK TIME: 12 MINUTES • TOTAL: 20 MINUTES SERVES: 2

Ingredients
1 tsp. pepper
2 C. almond milk
2 tbsp. almond flour
6 ounces ground sausage meat
1 tsp. pepper
1 tsp. salt
1 tsp. garlic powder
1 tsp. onion powder
1 C. panko breadcrumbs
1 C. almond flour
3 beaten eggs
6 ounces sirloin steak, pounded till thin

Directions:
1 **Preparing the Ingredients.** Season panko breadcrumbs with spices. Dredge steak in flour, then egg, and then seasoned panko mixture. Place into air fryer basket.
2 **Air Frying.** Set temperature to 370°F, and set time to 12 minutes. To make sausage gravy, cook sausage and drain off fat, but reserve 2 tablespoons. Add flour to sausage and mix until incorporated. Gradually mix in milk over medium to high heat till it becomes thick. Season mixture with pepper and cook 3 minutes longer. Serve steak topped with gravy and enjoy!

PER SERVING: CALORIES: 395; FAT: 11G; PROTEIN:39G; SUGAR:5G

Creamy Burger & Potato Bake

PREP: 5 MINUTES • COOK TIME: 55 MINUTES • TOTAL: 60 MINUTES SERVES: 3

Ingredients
salt to taste
freshly ground pepper, to taste
1/2 (10.75 ounce) can condensed cream of mushroom soup
1/2-pound lean ground beef
1-1/2 cups peeled and thinly sliced potatoes
1/2 cup shredded Cheddar cheese
1/4 cup chopped onion
1/4 cup and 2 tablespoons milk

Directions:
1 **Preparing the Ingredients.** Lightly grease baking pan of air fryer with cooking spray. Add ground beef. For 10 minutes, cook on 360°F. Stir and crumble halfway through cooking time.
Meanwhile, in a bowl, whisk well pepper, salt, milk, onion, and mushroom soup. Mix well.
Drain fat off ground beef and transfer beef to a plate.
In same air fryer baking pan, layer ½ of potatoes on bottom, then ½ of soup mixture, and then ½ of beef. Repeat process.
Cover pan with foil.
2 **Air Frying.** Cook for 30 minutes. Remove foil and cook for another 15 minutes or until potatoes are tender.
Serve and enjoy.

PER SERVING: CALORIES: 399; FAT: 26.9G; PROTEIN:22.1G

Beefy 'n Cheesy Spanish Rice Casserole

PREP: 10 MINUTES • COOK TIME: 50 MINUTES • TOTAL: 60 MINUTES
SERVES: 3

Ingredients

2 tablespoons chopped green bell pepper
1 tablespoon chopped fresh cilantro
1/2-pound lean ground beef
1/2 cup water
1/2 teaspoon salt
1/2 teaspoon brown sugar
1/2 pinch ground black pepper
1/3 cup uncooked long grain rice
1/4 cup finely chopped onion
1/4 cup chile sauce
1/4 teaspoon ground cumin
1/4 teaspoon Worcestershire sauce
1/4 cup shredded Cheddar cheese
1/2 (14.5 ounce) can canned tomatoes

Directions:

1 **Preparing the Ingredients.** Lightly grease baking pan of air fryer with cooking spray. Add ground beef.
2 **Air Frying.** For 10 minutes, cook on 360°F. Halfway through cooking time, stir and crumble beef. Discard excess fat,
Stir in pepper, Worcestershire sauce, cumin, brown sugar, salt, chile sauce, rice, water, tomatoes, green bell pepper, and onion. Mix well. Cover pan with foil and cook for 25 minutes. Stirring occasionally. Give it one last good stir, press down firmly and sprinkle cheese on top.
Cook uncovered for 15 minutes at 390°F until tops are lightly browned.
Serve and enjoy with chopped cilantro.

PER SERVING: CALORIES: 346; FAT: 19.1G; PROTEIN:18.5G

Warming Winter Beef with Celery

PREP: 5 MINUTES • COOK TIME: 12 MINUTES • TOTAL: 15 MINUTES
SERVES: 4

Ingredients

9 ounces tender beef, chopped
1/2 cup leeks, chopped
1/2 cup celery stalks, chopped
2 cloves garlic, smashed
2 tablespoons red cooking wine
3/4 cup cream of celery soup
2 sprigs rosemary, chopped
1/4 teaspoon smoked paprika
3/4 teaspoons salt
1/4 teaspoon black pepper, or to taste

Directions:

1 **Preparing the Ingredients.** Add the beef, leeks, celery, and garlic to the baking dish; cook for about 5 minutes at 390 degrees F. Once the meat is starting to tender, pour in the wine and soup. Season with rosemary, smoked paprika, salt, and black pepper. Now, cook an additional 7 minutes.

Beef & veggie Spring Rolls

PREP: 5 MINUTES • COOK TIME: 12 MINUTES • TOTAL: 55 MINUTES SERVES: 10

Ingredients

2-ounce Asian rice noodles
1 tablespoon sesame oil
7-ounce ground beef
1 small onion, chopped
3 garlic cloves, crushed
1 cup fresh mixed vegetables
1 teaspoon soy sauce
1 packet spring roll skins
2 tablespoons water
Olive oil, as required

Directions:

1 **Preparing the Ingredients.** Soak the noodles in warm water till soft.
   Drain and cut into small lengths. In a pan heat the oil and add the onion and garlic and sauté for about 4-5 minutes.
   Add beef and cook for about 4-5 minutes.
   Add vegetables and cook for about 5-7 minutes or till cooked through.
   Stir in soy sauce and remove from the heat.
   Immediately, stir in the noodles and keep aside till all the juices have been absorbed.
   Preheat the Chefman air fryer to 350 degrees F. and preheat the oven to 350 degrees F also.
   Place the spring rolls skin onto a smooth surface.
   Add a line of the filling diagonally across.
   Fold the top point over the filling and then fold in both sides.
   On the final point brush it with water before rolling to seal.
   Brush the spring rolls with oil.
2 **Air Frying**. Arrange the rolls in batches in the Chefman air fryer and Cook for about 8 minutes.

Repeat with remaining rolls.
Now, place spring rolls onto a baking sheet.
Bake for about 6 minutes per side.

Charred Onions And Steak Cube BBQ

PREP: 5 MINUTES • COOK TIME: 40 MINUTES • TOTAL: 45 MINUTES
SERVES: 3

Ingredients

1 cup red onions, cut into wedges
1 tablespoon dry mustard
1 tablespoon olive oil
1-pound boneless beef sirloin, cut into cubes
Salt and pepper to taste

Directions:

1   **Preparing the Ingredients.** Preheat the Chefman air fryer to 390°F.
    Place the grill pan accessory in the air fryer.
    Toss all ingredients in a bowl and mix until everything is coated with the seasonings.
2   **Air Frying**. Place on the grill pan and cook for 40 minutes.
    Halfway through the cooking time, give a stir to cook evenly.

PER SERVING: CALORIES: 260; FAT: 10.7G; PROTEIN:35.5G

Beef Stroganoff

PREP: 10 MINUTES • COOK TIME: 14 MINUTES • TOTAL: 24 MINUTES
SERVES: 4

Ingredients

9 Ozs Tender Beef
1 Onion, chopped
1 Tbsp Paprika
3/4 Cup Sour Cream
Salt and Pepper to taste
 Baking Dish

Directions:

Preparing the Ingredients. Preheat the Chefman air fryer to 390 degrees.
Chop the beef and marinate it with the paprika.
Add the chopped onions into the baking dish and heat for about 2 minutes in the Chefman air fryer.
When the onions are transparent, add the beef into the dish and cook for 5 minutes.
Once the beef is starting to tender, pour in the sour cream and cook for another 7 minutes.
At this point, the liquid should have reduced. Season with salt and pepper and serve.

Cheesy Ground Beef And Mac Taco Casserole

PREP: 10 MINUTES • **COOK TIME:** 25 MINUTES • **TOTAL:** 35 MINUTES
SERVES: 5

Ingredients
1-ounce shredded Cheddar cheese
1-ounce shredded Monterey Jack cheese
2 tablespoons chopped green onions
1/2 (10.75 ounce) can condensed tomato soup
1/2-pound lean ground beef
1/2 cup crushed tortilla chips
1/4-pound macaroni, cooked according to manufacturer's Instructions
1/4 cup chopped onion
1/4 cup sour cream (optional)
1/2 (1.25 ounce) package taco seasoning mix
1/2 (14.5 ounce) can diced tomatoes

Directions:
1   **Preparing the Ingredients.** Lightly grease baking pan of air fryer with cooking spray. Add onion and ground beef. For 10 minutes, cook on 360°F. Halfway through cooking time, stir and crumble ground beef.
Add taco seasoning, diced tomatoes, and tomato soup. Mix well. Mix in pasta.
Sprinkle crushed tortilla chips. Sprinkle cheese.
2   **Air Frying**. Cook for 15 minutes at 390°F until tops are lightly browned and cheese is melted.
Serve and enjoy.

PER SERVING: CALORIES: 329; FAT: 17G; PROTEIN:15.6G

Beefy Steak Topped with Chimichurri Sauce

PREP: 5 MINUTES • **COOK TIME:** 60 MINUTES • **TOTAL:** 65 MINUTES
SERVES: 6

Ingredients
1 cup commercial chimichurri
3 pounds steak
Salt and pepper to taste

Directions:
1   **Preparing the Ingredients.** Place all ingredients in a Ziploc bag and marinate in the fridge for 2 hours.
Preheat the air fryer to 390°F.
Place the grill pan accessory in the air fryer.
2   **Air Frying**. Grill the skirt steak for 20 minutes per batch.
Flip the steak every 10 minutes for even grilling.

PER SERVING: CALORIES: 507; FAT: 27G; PROTEIN:63 G

Beef Ribeye Steak

PREP: 5 MINUTES • COOK TIME: 20 MINUTES • TOTAL: 25 MINUTES
SERVES: 4

Ingredients

4 (8-ounce) ribeye steaks
1 tablespoon McCormick Grill Mates Montreal Steak Seasoning
Salt
Pepper

Directions:

1 **Preparing the Ingredients.** Season the steaks with the steak seasoning and salt and pepper to taste. Place 2 steaks in the Chefman air fryer. You can use an accessory grill pan, a layer rack, or the standard Chefman air fryer basket.

2 **Air Frying**. Cook for 4 minutes. Open the Chefman air fryer and flip the steaks. Cook for an additional 4 to 5 minutes. Check for doneness to determine how much additional cook time is need. Remove the cooked steaks from the Chefman air fryer, then repeat steps 2 through 4 for the remaining 2 steaks. Cool before serving.

PER SERVING: CALORIES: 293; FAT: 22G; PROTEIN:23G; FIBER:0G

Air Fryer Roast Beef

PREP: 5 MINUTES • COOK TIME: 45 MINUTES • TOTAL: 50 MINUTES
SERVES: 6

Ingredients

Roast beef
1 tbsp. olive oil
Seasonings of choice

Directions:

1 **Preparing the Ingredients.** Ensure your Chefman air fryer is preheated to 160 degrees.
   Place roast in bowl and toss with olive oil and desired seasonings.
   Put seasoned roast into air fryer.

2 **Air Frying**. Set temperature to 160°F, and set time to 30 minutes and cook 30 minutes.
   Turn roast when the timer sounds and cook another 15 minutes.

PER SERVING: CALORIES: 267; FAT: 8G; PROTEIN:21G; SUGAR:1G

Beef Korma

PREP: 10 MINUTES • COOK TIME: 20 MINUTES • TOTAL: 30 MINUTES
SERVES: 6

Ingredients
½ cup yogurt
1 tablespoon curry powder
1 tablespoon olive oil
1 onion, chopped
2 cloves garlic, minced
1 tomato, diced
½ cup frozen baby peas, thawed

Directions:
1 **Preparing the Ingredients.** In a medium bowl, combine the steak, yogurt, and curry powder. Stir and set aside.
In a 6-inch metal bowl, combine the olive oil, onion, and garlic.
2 **Air Frying.** Cook for 3 to 4 minutes or until crisp and tender.
Add the steak along with the yogurt and the diced tomato. Cook for 12 to 13 minutes or until steak is almost tender. Stir in the peas and cook for 2 to 3 minutes or until hot.

PER SERVING: CALORIES: 289; FAT: 11G; PROTEIN:38G; FIBER:2G

Cumin-Paprika Rubbed Beef Brisket

PREP: 5 MINUTES • COOK TIME: 2 HOURS • TOTAL: 2 HOURS, 5 MINUTES
SERVES: 12

Ingredients
¼ teaspoon cayenne pepper
1 ½ tablespoons paprika
1 teaspoon garlic powder
1 teaspoon ground cumin
1 teaspoon onion powder
2 teaspoons dry mustard
2 teaspoons ground black pepper
2 teaspoons salt
5 pounds brisket roast
5 tablespoons olive oil

Directions:
1 **Preparing the Ingredients**. Place all ingredients in a Ziploc bag and allow to marinate in the fridge for at least 2 hours. Preheat the air fryer for 5 minutes.
Place the meat in a baking dish that will fit in the air fryer.
2 **Air Frying.** Place in the air fryer and cook for 2 hours at 350°F.

PER SERVING: CALORIES: 269; FAT: 12.8G; PROTEIN:35.6G; FIBER:2G

Chili-Espresso Marinated Steak

PREP: 5 MINUTES • COOK TIME: 50 MINUTES• TOTAL: 55 MINUTES
SERVES: 3

Ingredients
½ teaspoon garlic powder
1 ½ pounds beef flank steak
1 teaspoon instant espresso powder
2 tablespoons olive oil
2 teaspoons chili powder
Salt and pepper to taste

Directions:
1   **Preparing the Ingredients**. Preheat the Chefman air fryer to 390°F.
    Place the grill pan accessory in the air fryer.
    Make the dry rub by mixing the chili powder, salt, pepper, espresso powder, and garlic powder.
    Rub all over the steak and brush with oil.
2   **Air Frying.** Place on the grill pan and cook for 40 minutes.
    Halfway through the cooking time, flip the beef to cook evenly.

PER SERVING: CALORIES: 249; FAT: 17G; PROTEIN:20G; FIBER:2G

Sugar-And-Spice Beef Empanadas

PREP: 15 MINUTES • COOK TIME: 15 MINUTES • TOTAL: 30 MINUTES
SERVES: 4

Ingredients
6 ounces of raw, lean ground beef
¼ cup of raw white onions, sliced and finely diced
1 teaspoon of cinnamon
½ teaspoon of nutmeg
½ teaspoon of ground cloves
1 small pinch of brown sugar
2 teaspoons of red chilli powder
pre-made empanada dough shells

Directions:
1   **Preparing the Ingredients.** In a deep stovetop saucepan, crumble and cook the ground beef at medium heat. Add in the onions, stirring continuously with a wooden spoon, then add the cinnamon, nutmeg and cloves. Break up the ground beef as it cooks, so it doesn't form large clumps. Remove the saucepan from the stovetop as soon as the beef is fully cooked, the onions are soft, and the spices are releasing their fragrances. Do not overcook, you want the meat to remain moist and juicy. Cover the saucepan and let stand on a heatsafe surface for a few minutes. Lay empanada shells flat on a clean counter. Spoon the spiced cooked beef from the saucepan into the empanada shells – a heaping spoonful on each, though not so much that the mixture spills over the edges. Fold the empanada shells over so that the spiced beef is fully covered. Seal edges with water and press down with a fork to secure. Sprinkle brown sugar over the still-wet seams of the empanadas, for an extra sweet crunch. Cover the basket of the Chefman air

fryerwith a lining of tin foil, leaving the edges uncovered to allow air to circulate through the basket.

2 **Air Frying.** Place the empanadas in the foil-lined Chefman air fryer basket and set at 350 degrees for 15 minutes. Halfway through, slide the frying basket out and flip the empanadas using a spatula. Remove when golden, and serve directly from the basket onto plates.

Crispy Mongolian Beef

PREP: 5 MINUTES • COOK TIME: 10 MINUTES • TOTAL: 15 MINUTES SERVES: 6

Ingredients
Olive oil
½ C. almond flour
2 pounds beef tenderloin or beef chuck, sliced into strips
Sauce:
½ C. chopped green onion
1 tsp. red chili flakes
1 tsp. almond flour
½ C. brown sugar
1 tsp. hoisin sauce
½ C. water
½ C. rice vinegar
½ C. low-sodium soy sauce
1 tbsp. chopped garlic
1 tbsp. finely chopped ginger
2 tbsp. olive oil

Directions:
1 **Preparing the Ingredients.** Toss strips of beef in almond flour, ensuring they are coated well. Add to the Chefman air fryer.

2 **Air Frying**. Set temperature to 300°F, and set time to 10 minutes, and cook 10 minutes at 300 degrees.
   Meanwhile, add all sauce ingredients to the pan and bring to a boil. Mix well.
   Add beef strips to the sauce and cook 2 minutes.
   Serve over cauliflower rice!

PER SERVING: CALORIES: 290; FAT: 14G; PROTEIN:22G; SUGAR:1G

Beef & Lemon Schnitzel for One

PREP: 5 MINUTES • COOK TIME: 12 MINUTES • TOTAL: 17 MINUTES
SERVES: 1

Ingredients
2 Tbsp Oil
2–3 oz Breadcrumbs
1 Whisked Egg in a Saucer/Soup Plate
1 Beef Schnitzel
1 Freshly Picked Lemon

Directions:
1   **Preparing the Ingredients.** Mix the oil and breadcrumbs together until loose and crumbly. Dip the meat into the egg, then into the crumbs. Make sure that it is evenly covered.
2   **Air Frying**. Gently place in the Chefman air fryer basket, and cook at 350° F (preheat if needed) until done. The timing will depend on the thickness of the schnitzel, but for a relatively thin one, it should take roughly 12 min. Serve with a lemon half and a garden salad.

Crispy Beef Schnitzel

PREP: 5 MINUTES • COOK TIME: 12 MINUTES • TOTAL: 17 MINUTES
SERVES: 1

Ingredients
1 beef schnitzel
Salt and ground black pepper, to taste
2 tablespoons olive oil
1/3 cup breadcrumbs
1 egg, whisked

Directions:
Preparing the Ingredients. Season the schnitzel with salt and black pepper.
In a mixing bowl, combine the oil and breadcrumbs. In another shallow bowl, beat the egg until frothy.
Dip the schnitzel in the egg; then, dip it in the oil mixture.
Air-fry at 350 degrees F for 12 minutes.
Enjoy!

Simple Steak

PREP: 6MINUTES • COOK TIME: 14 MINUTES • TOTAL: 20 MINUTES
SERVES: 2

Ingredients
½ pound quality cuts steak
Salt and freshly ground black pepper, to taste

Directions:
1. **Preparing the Ingredients.** Preheat the Chefman air fryer to 390 degrees F.
   Rub the steak with salt and pepper evenly.
2. **Air Frying.** Place the steak in the Chefman air fryer basket and cook for about 14 minutes crispy.

Garlic-Cumin And Orange Juice Marinated Steak

PREP: 6 MINUTES • COOK TIME: 60 MINUTES • TOTAL: 66 MINUTES
SERVES: 4

Ingredients
¼ cup orange juice
1 teaspoon ground cumin
2 pounds skirt steak, trimmed from excess fat
2 tablespoons lime juice
2 tablespoons olive oil
4 cloves of garlic, minced
Salt and pepper to taste

Directions:
1. **Preparing the Ingredients.** Place all ingredients in a mixing bowl and allow to marinate in the fridge for at least 2 hours
   Preheat the air fryer to 390°F.
   Place the grill pan accessory in the air fryer.
2. **Air Frying.** Grill for 15 minutes per batch and flip the beef every 8 minutes for even grilling.
   Meanwhile, pour the marinade on a saucepan and allow to simmer for 10 minutes or until the sauce thickens.
   Slice the beef and pour over the sauce.

PER SERVING: CALORIES: 568; FAT: 34.7G; PROTEIN:59.1G; SUGAR:1G

Beef Taco Fried Egg Rolls

PREP: 10 MINUTES • COOK TIME: 12 MINUTES • TOTAL: 25 MINUTES
SERVES: 8

Ingredients

1 tsp. cilantro
2 chopped garlic cloves
1 tbsp. olive oil
1 C. shredded Mexican cheese
½ packet taco seasoning
½ can cilantro lime rotel
½ chopped onion
16 egg roll wrappers
1 pound lean ground beef

Directions:

1 **Preparing the Ingredients.** Ensure that your Chefman air fryer is preheated to 400 degrees.
   Add onions and garlic to a skillet, cooking till fragrant. Then add taco seasoning, pepper, salt, and beef, cooking till beef is broke up into tiny pieces and cooked thoroughly.
   Add rotel and stir well.
   Lay out egg wrappers and brush with water to soften a bit.
   Load wrappers with beef filling and add cheese to each.
   Fold diagonally to close and use water to secure edges.
   Brush filled egg wrappers with olive oil and add to the air fryer.
2 **Air Frying**. Set temperature to 400°F, and set time to 8 minutes. Cook 8 minutes, flip, and cook another 4 minutes.
   Served sprinkled with cilantro.

PER SERVING: CALORIES: 348; FAT: 11G; PROTEIN:24G; SUGAR:1G

Beef With Beans

PREP: 10 MINUTES • COOK TIME: 13 MINUTES • TOTAL: 23 MINUTES
SERVES: 8

Ingredients

12 Ozs Lean Steak
1 Onion, sliced
1 Can Chopped Tomatoes
3/4 Cup Beef Stock
4 Tsp Fresh Thyme, chopped
1 Can Red Kidney Beans
Salt and Pepper to taste
Oven Safe Bowl

Directions:

1. **Preparing the Ingredients.** Preheat the Chefman air fryer to 390 degrees.
   Trim the fat from the meat and cut into thin 1cm strips
   Add onion slices to the oven safe bowl and place in the Chefman air fryer.
2. **Air Frying**. Cook for 3 minutes. Add the meat and continue cooking for 5 minutes. Add the tomatoes and their juice, beef stock, thyme and the beans and cook for an additional 5 minutes
   Season with black pepper to taste.

Swedish Meatballs

PREP: 10 MINUTES • COOK TIME: 14 MINUTES • TOTAL: 24 MINUTES
SERVES: 4

PER SERVING: CALORIES: 178; FAT: 14G; PROTEIN:9G; FIBER:0G

Ingredients

For the meatballs

1 pound 93% lean ground beef
1 (1-ounce) packet Lipton Onion Recipe Soup & Dip Mix
⅓ cup bread crumbs
1 egg, beaten
Salt
Pepper

For the gravy

1 cup beef broth
⅓ cup heavy cream
3   tablespoons all-purpose flour

Directions:

1   **Preparing the Ingredients.** In a large bowl, combine the ground beef, onion soup mix, bread crumbs, egg, and salt and pepper to taste. Mix thoroughly.

Using 2 tablespoons of the meat mixture, create each meatball by rolling the beef mixture around in your hands. This should yield about 10 meatballs.

2   **Air Frying**. Place the meatballs in the Chefman air fryer. It is okay to stack them. Cook for 14 minutes.

While the meatballs cook, prepare the gravy. Heat a saucepan over medium-high heat.

Add the beef broth and heavy cream. Stir for 1 to 2 minutes.

Add the flour and stir. Cover and allow the sauce to simmer for 3 to 4 minutes, or until thick.

Drizzle the gravy over the meatballs and serve.

Rice and Meatball Stuffed Bell Peppers

PREP: 13 MINUTES • COOK TIME: 15 MINUTES • TOTAL: 28 MINUTES
SERVES: 4

Ingredients
4 bell peppers
1 tablespoon olive oil
1 small onion, chopped
2 cloves garlic, minced
1 cup frozen cooked rice, thawed
16 to 20 small frozen precooked meatballs, thawed
½ cup tomato sauce
3 tablespoons Dijon mustard

Directions:
1 **Preparing the Ingredients.** To prepare the peppers, cut off about ½ inch of the tops. Carefully remove the membranes and seeds from inside the peppers. Set aside.
   In a 6-by-6-by-2-inch pan, combine the olive oil, onion, and garlic.
2 **Air Frying**. Bake in the Chefman air fryer for 2 to 4 minutes or until crisp and tender. Remove the vegetable mixture from the pan and set aside in a medium bowl.
   Add the rice, meatballs, tomato sauce, and mustard to the vegetable mixture and stir to combine. Stuff the peppers with the meat-vegetable mixture.
   Place the peppers in the air fryer basket and bake for 9 to 13 minutes or until the filling is hot and the peppers are tender.

PER SERVING: CALORIES: 487; FAT: 21G; PROTEIN:26G; FIBER:6G

Pub Style Corned Beef Egg Rolls

PREP: 15 MINUTES • COOK TIME: 10 MINUTES • TOTAL: 35 MINUTES
SERVES: 10

Ingredients
Olive oil
½ C. orange marmalade
5 slices of Swiss cheese
4 C. corned beef and cabbage
1 egg
10 egg roll wrappers
Brandy Mustard Sauce:
1/16th tsp. pepper
2 tbsp. whole grain mustard
1 tsp. dry mustard powder
1 C. heavy cream
½ C. chicken stock
¼ C. brandy
¾ C. dry white wine
¼ tsp. curry powder
½ tbsp. cilantro
1 minced shallot
2 tbsp. ghee

Directions:
1 **Preparing the Ingredients.** To make mustard sauce, add shallots and ghee to skillet, cooking until softened. Then add brandy and wine, heating to a low boil. Cook 5 minutes for liquids to reduce. Add stock and seasonings. Simmer 5 minutes. Turn down heat and add heavy cream. Cook on low till sauce reduces and it covers the back of a spoon.
   Place sauce in the fridge to chill.
   Crack the egg in a bowl and set to the side. Lay out an egg wrapper with the corner towards you. Brush the edges with egg wash.
   Place 1/3 cup of corned beef mixture into the center along with 2 tablespoons of marmalade and ½ a slice of Swiss cheese.

Fold the bottom corner over filling. As you are folding the sides, make sure they are stick well to the first flap you made. Place filled rolls into prepared air fryer basket. Spritz rolls with olive oil.

2 **Air Frying**. Set temperature to 390°F, and set time to 10 minutes. Cook 10 minutes at 390 degrees, shaking halfway through cooking.
Serve rolls with Brandy Mustard sauce.

PER SERVING: CALORIES: 415; FAT: 13G; PROTEIN:38G; SUGAR:4G

Stir-Fried Steak and Cabbage
PREP: 15 MINUTES • COOK TIME: 10 MINUTES • TOTAL: 35 MINUTES SERVES: 4

Ingredients
½ pound sirloin steak, cut into strips
2 teaspoons cornstarch
1 tablespoon peanut oil
2 cups chopped red or green cabbage
1 yellow bell pepper, chopped
2 green onions, chopped
2 cloves garlic, sliced
½ cup commercial stir-fry sauce

Directions:
1 **Preparing the Ingredients.** Toss the steak with the cornstarch and set aside.
In a 6-inch metal bowl, combine the peanut oil with the cabbage.
2 **Air Frying**. Place in the basket and cook for 3 to 4 minutes.
Remove the bowl from the basket and add the steak, pepper, onions, and garlic. Return to the Chefman air fryer and cook for 3 to 5 minutes or until the steak is cooked to desired doneness and vegetables are crisp and tender.
Add the stir-fry sauce and cook for 2 to 4 minutes or until hot. Serve over rice.

PER SERVING: CALORIES: 180; FAT: 7G; PROTEIN:20G; FIBER:2G

Reuben Egg Rolls

PREP: 5 MINUTES • COOK TIME: 20 MINUTES • TOTAL: 25 MINUTES
SERVES: 6

Ingredients
Swiss cheese
Can of sauerkraut
Sliced deli corned beef
Egg roll wrappers

Directions:

1 **Preparing the Ingredients.** Cut corned beef and Swiss cheese into thin slices. Drain sauerkraut and dry well.
Take egg roll wrapper and moisten edges with water.
Stack center with corned beef and cheese till you reach desired thickness. Top off with sauerkraut.
Fold corner closest to you over the edge of filling. Bring up sides and glue with water.
Add to the Chefman air fryer basket and spritz with olive oil.

2 **Air Frying.** Set temperature to 400°F, and set time to 4 minutes. Cook 4 minutes at 400 degrees, then flip and cook another 4 minutes.

PER SERVING: CALORIES: 251; FAT: 12G; PROTEIN:31G; SUGAR:4G

Air-Fried Philly Cheesesteak

PREP: 5 MINUTES • COOK TIME: 16 MINUTES • TOTAL: 21 MINUTES
SERVES: 6

Ingredients
Large hoagie bun, sliced in half
6 ounces of sirloin or flank steak, sliced into bite-sized pieces
½ white onion, rinsed and sliced
½ red pepper, rinsed and sliced
slices of American cheese

Directions:

1 **Preparing the Ingredients**. Set the Chefman air fryer to 320 degrees for 10 minutes.
Arrange the steak pieces, onions and peppers on a piece of tin foil, flat and not overlapping, and set the tin foil on one side of the air-fryer basket. The foil should not take up more than half of the surface; the juices from the steak and the moisture from the vegetables will mingle while cooking.
Lay the hoagie-bun halves, crusty-side up and soft-side down, on the other half of the Chefman air fryer.

2 **Air Frying**. After 10 minutes, the air fryer will shut off; the hoagie buns should be starting to crisp and the steak and vegetables will have begun to cook.
Carefully, flip the hoagie buns so they are now crusty-side down and soft-side up; cover both sides with one slice each of American cheese.
With a long spoon, gently stir the steak, onions and peppers in the foil to ensure even coverage.
Set the air fryer to 360 degrees for 6 minutes.
After 6 minutes, when the fryer shuts off, the cheese will be perfectly melted over

the toasted bread, and the steak will be juicy on the inside and crispy on the outside.

Remove the cheesy hoagie halves first, using tongs, and set on a serving plate; then cover one side with the steak, and top with the onions and peppers. Close with the other cheesy hoagie-half, slice into two pieces, and enjoy.

Herbed Roast Beef

PREP: 5 MINUTES • COOK TIME: 20 MINUTES • TOTAL: 25 MINUTES SERVES: 6

Ingredients

½ tsp. fresh rosemary
1 tsp. dried thyme
¼ tsp. pepper
1 tsp. salt
4-pound top round roast beef
tsp. olive oil

Directions:

1. **Preparing the Ingredients.** Ensure your air fryer is preheated to 360 degrees.
   Rub olive oil all over beef.
   Mix rosemary, thyme, pepper, and salt together and proceed to rub all sides of beef with spice mixture.
   Place seasoned beef into air fryer.
2. **Air Frying**. Set temperature to 360°F, and set time to 20 minutes.
   Allow roast to rest 10 minutes before slicing to serve.

PER SERVING: CALORIES: 502; FAT: 18G; PROTEIN:48G; SUGAR:2G

Tender Beef with Sour Cream Sauce

PREP: 5 MINUTES • COOK TIME: 12 MINUTES • TOTAL: 17 MINUTES
SERVES: 2

Ingredients

9 ounces tender beef, chopped
1 cup scallions, chopped
2 cloves garlic, smashed
3/4 cup sour cream
3/4 teaspoon salt
1/4 teaspoon black pepper, or to taste
1/2 teaspoon dried dill weed

Directions:

1 **Preparing the Ingredients.** Add the beef, scallions, and garlic to the baking dish.
2 **Air Frying.** Cook for about 5 minutes at 390 degrees F.
   Once the meat is starting to tender, pour in the sour cream. Stir in the salt, black pepper, and dill.
   Now, cook 7 minutes longer.

Beef Empanadas

PREP: 5 MINUTES • COOK TIME: 20 MINUTES • TOTAL: 25 MINUTES
SERVES: 6

Ingredients

1 tsp. water
1 egg white
1 C. picadillo
8 Goya empanada discs (thawed)

Directions:

1 **Preparing the Ingredients.** Ensure your air fryer is preheated to 325. Spray basket with olive oil.
   Place 2 tablespoons of picadillo into the center of each disc. Fold disc in half and use a fork to seal edges. Repeat with all ingredients.
   Whisk egg white with water and brush tops of empanadas with egg wash.
   Add 2-3 empanadas to the Chefman air fryer.
2 **Air Frying.** Set temperature to 325°F, and set time to 8 minutes, cook until golden. Repeat till you cook all filled empanadas.

PER SERVING: CALORIES: 183; FAT: 5G; PROTEIN:11G; SUGAR:2G

Beef Pot Pie

PREP: 5 MINUTES • COOK TIME: 90 MINUTES • TOTAL: 95 MINUTES
SERVES: 2

Ingredients

1 tablespoon olive oil
1 pound beef stewing steak, cubed
1 large onion, chopped
1 tablespoon tomato puree
1 can ale
Warm water, as required
2 beef bouillon cubes
Salt and freshly ground black pepper, to taste
1 tablespoon plain flour plus more for dusting
1 prepared short crust pastry

Directions:

1 **Preparing the Ingredients.** In a pan, heat oil on medium heat. Add steak and cook for about 4-5 minutes. Add onion and cook for about 4-5 minutes.

Add tomato puree and cook for about 2-3 minutes.

In a jug, add the ale and enough water to double the mixture.

Add the ale mixture, cubes, salt and black pepper in the pan with beef and bring to a boil on high heat. Reduce the heat to low and simmer for about 1 hour.

In a bowl, mix together flour and 3 tablespoons of warm water.

Slowly, add the flour mixture in beef mixture, stirring continuously.

Remove from heat and keep aside. Roll out the short crust pastry.

Line 2 ramekins with pastry and dust with flour.

Divide the beef mixture in the ramekins evenly.

Place extra pastry on top.

2 **Air Frying.** Preheat the Chefman air fryer to 390 degrees F, and Cook for about 10 minutes.

Now, set the Chefman air fryer to 335 degrees F, and Cook for about 6 minutes more.

Bolognaise Sauce

PREP: 5 MINUTES • COOK TIME: 30 MINUTES • TOTAL: 35 MINUTES
SERVES: 2

Ingredients
13 Ozs Ground Beef
1 Carrot
1 Stalk of Celery
10 Ozs Diced Tomatoes
1/2 Onion
Salt and Pepper to taste
Oven safe bowl

Directions:
1. **Preparing the Ingredients.** Preheat the Chefman air fryer to 390 degrees.
   Finely dice the carrot, celery and onions. Place into the oven safe bowl along with the ground beef and combine well
2. **Air Frying.** Place the bowl into the Chefman air fryer tray and cook for 12 minutes until browned.
   Pour the diced tomatoes into the bowl and replace in the Chefman air fryer.
   Season with salt and pepper, then cook for another 18 minutes
   Serve over cooked pasta or freeze for later use.

Breaded Spam Steaks

PREP: 5 MINUTES • COOK TIME: 5 MINUTES • TOTAL: 10 MINUTES
SERVES: 2

Ingredients
12 Oz Can Luncheon Meat
1 Cup All Purpose Flour
2 Eggs, beaten
2 Cups Italian Seasoned Breadcrumbs

Directions:
1. **Preparing the Ingredients.** Preheat the Chefman air fryer to 380 degrees.
   Cut the luncheon meat into 1/4 inch slices. Gently press the luncheon meat slices into the flour to coat and shake off the excess flour. Dip into the beaten egg, then press into breadcrumbs.
2. **Air Frying.** Place the battered slices into the Chefman air fryer tray and cook for 3 to 5 minutes until golden brown.
   Serve with chili or tomato sauce

Air Fryer Burgers

PREP: 5 MINUTES • COOK TIME: 10 MINUTES • TOTAL: 15 MINUTES
SERVES: 4

Ingredients
1 pound lean ground beef
1 tsp. dried parsley
½ tsp. dried oregano
½ tsp. pepper
½ tsp. salt
½ tsp. onion powder
½ tsp. garlic powder
Few drops of liquid smoke
1 tsp. Worcestershire sauce

Directions:
1 **Preparing the Ingredients.** Ensure your air fryer is preheated to 350 degrees. Mix all seasonings together till combined. Place beef in a bowl and add seasonings. Mix well, but do not overmix. Make 4 patties from the mixture and using your thumb, making an indent in the center of each patty. Add patties to air fryer basket.
2 **Air Frying.** Set temperature to 350°F, and set time to 10 minutes, and cook 10 minutes. No need to turn.

PER SERVING: CALORIES: 148; FAT: 5G; PROTEIN:24G; SUGAR:1G

Cheese-Stuffed Meatballs

PREP: 10 MINUTES • COOK TIME: 10 MINUTES • TOTAL: 20 MINUTES
SERVES: 4

Ingredients
⅓ cup soft bread crumbs
3 tablespoons milk
1 tablespoon ketchup
1 egg
½ teaspoon dried marjoram
Pinch salt
Freshly ground black pepper
1 pound 95 percent lean ground beef
20 ½-inch cubes of cheese
Olive oil for misting

Directions:
1 **Preparing the Ingredients.** In a large bowl, combine the bread crumbs, milk, ketchup, egg, marjoram, salt, and pepper, and mix well. Add the ground beef and mix gently but thoroughly with your hands. Form the mixture into 20 meatballs. Shape each meatball around a cheese cube. Mist the meatballs with olive oil and put into the Chefman air fryer basket.
2 **Air Frying.** Bake for 10 to 13 minutes or until the meatballs register 165°F on a meat thermometer.

PER SERVING: CALORIES: 393; FAT: 17G; PROTEIN:50G; FIBER:0G

Roasted Stuffed Peppers

PREP: 5 MINUTES • COOK TIME: 20 MINUTES • TOTAL: 25 MINUTES
SERVES: 4

Ingredients

4 ounces shredded cheddar cheese
½ tsp. pepper
½ tsp. salt
1 tsp. Worcestershire sauce
½ C. tomato sauce
8 ounces lean ground beef
1 tsp. olive oil
1 minced garlic clove
½ chopped onion
2 green peppers

Directions:

1 **Preparing the Ingredients.** Ensure your air fryer is preheated to 390 degrees. Spray with olive oil.
Cut stems off bell peppers and remove seeds. Cook in boiling salted water for 3 minutes.
Sauté garlic and onion together in a skillet until golden in color.
Take skillet off the heat. Mix pepper, salt, Worcestershire sauce, ¼ cup of tomato sauce, half of cheese and beef together.
Divide meat mixture into pepper halves.
Top filled peppers with remaining cheese and tomato sauce.
Place filled peppers in the Chefman air fryer.

2 **Air Frying.** Set temperature to 390°F, and set time to 20 minutes, bake 15-20 minutes.

PER SERVING: CALORIES: 295; FAT: 8G; PROTEIN:23G; SUGAR:2G

Air Fried Steak Sandwich

PREP: 5 MINUTES • COOK TIME: 16 MINUTES • TOTAL: 21 MINUTES
SERVES: 4

Ingredients

Large hoagie bun, sliced in half
6 ounces of sirloin or flank steak, sliced into bite-sized pieces
½ tablespoon of mustard powder
½ tablespoon of soy sauce
1 tablespoon of fresh bleu cheese, crumbled
8 medium-sized cherry tomatoes, sliced in half
1 cup of fresh arugula, rinsed and patted dry

Directions:

1 **Preparing the Ingredients.** In a small mixing bowl, combine the soy sauce and onion powder; stir with a fork until thoroughly combined.
Lay the raw steak strips in the soy-mustard mixture, and fully immerse each piece to marinate.
Set the Chefman air fryer to 320 degrees for 10 minutes.
Arrange the soy-mustard marinated steak pieces on a piece of tin foil, flat and not overlapping, and set the tin foil on one side of the Chefman air fryer basket. The foil should not take up more than half of the surface.
Lay the hoagie-bun halves, crusty-side up and soft-side down, on the other half of the air-fryer.

2 **Air Frying.** After 10 minutes, the Chefman air fryer will shut off; the hoagie buns should be starting to crisp and the steak will have begun to cook.
Carefully, flip the hoagie buns so they are now crusty-side down and soft-side up; crumble a layer of the bleu cheese on each hoagie half.

With a long spoon, gently stir the marinated steak in the foil to ensure even coverage.

Set the air fryer to 360 degrees for 6 minutes.

After 6 minutes, when the fryer shuts off, the bleu cheese will be perfectly melted over the toasted bread, and the steak will be juicy on the inside and crispy on the outside.

Remove the cheesy hoagie halves first, using tongs, and set on a serving plate; then cover one side with the steak, and top with the cherry-tomato halves and the arugula. Close with the other cheesy hoagie-half, slice into two pieces, and enjoy.

Carrot and Beef Cocktail Balls

PREP: 5 MINUTES • COOK TIME: 20 MINUTES • TOTAL: 25 MINUTES
SERVES: 10

Ingredients

1 pound ground beef
2 carrots
1 red onion, peeled and chopped
2 cloves garlic
1/2 teaspoon dried rosemary, crushed
1/2 teaspoon dried basil
1 teaspoon dried oregano
1 egg
3/4 cup breadcrumbs
1/2 teaspoon salt
1/2 teaspoon black pepper, or to taste
1 cup plain flour

Directions:

1 **Preparing the Ingredients**. Place ground beef in a large bowl. In a food processor, pulse the carrot, onion and garlic; transfer the vegetable mixture to a large-sized bowl.

   Then, add the rosemary, basil, oregano, egg, breadcrumbs, salt, and black pepper.

   Shape the mixture into even balls; refrigerate for about 30 minutes. Roll the balls into the flour.

2 **Air Frying**. Then, air-fry the balls at 350 degrees F for about 20 minutes, turning occasionally; work with batches. Serve with toothpicks.

Beef Steaks with Beans

PREP: 5 MINUTES • COOK TIME: 10 MINUTES • TOTAL: 15 MINUTES SERVES: 4

Ingredients

4 beef steaks, trim the fat and cut into strips
1 cup green onions, chopped
2 cloves garlic, minced
1 red bell pepper, seeded and thinly sliced
1 can tomatoes, crushed
1 can cannellini beans
3/4 cup beef broth
1/4 teaspoon dried basil
1/2 teaspoon cayenne pepper
1/2 teaspoon sea salt
1/4 teaspoon ground black pepper, or to taste

Directions:

1 **Preparing the Ingredients**. Add the steaks, green onions and garlic to the Chefman air fryer basket.

2 **Air Frying**. Cook at 390 degrees F for 10 minutes, working in batches.
Stir in the remaining ingredients and cook for an additional 5 minutes.

Air Fryer Beef Steak

PREP: 5 MINUTES • COOK TIME: 15 MINUTES • TOTAL: 20 MINUTES
SERVES: 4

Ingredients

1 tbsp. olive oil
Pepper and salt
2 pounds of ribeye steak

Directions:

1 **Preparing the Ingredients.** Season meat on both sides with pepper and salt. Rub all sides of meat with olive oil. Preheat air fryer to 356 degrees and spritz with olive oil.

2 **Air Frying**. Set temperature to 356°F, and set time to 7 minutes. Cook steak 7 minutes. Flip and cook an additional 6 minutes.
   Let meat sit 2-5 minutes to rest. Slice and serve with salad.

PER SERVING: CALORIES: 233; FAT: 19G; PROTEIN:16G; SUGAR:0G

Mushroom Meatloaf

PREP: 5 MINUTES • COOK TIME: 25 MINUTES • TOTAL: 30 MINUTES
SERVES: 4

Ingredients

14-ounce lean ground beef
1 chorizo sausage, chopped finely
1 small onion, chopped
1 garlic clove, minced
2 tablespoons fresh cilantro, chopped
3 tablespoons breadcrumbs
1 egg
Salt and freshly ground black pepper, to taste
2 tablespoons fresh mushrooms, sliced thinly
3 tablespoons olive oil

Directions:

1 **Preparing the Ingredients.** Preheat the Air fryer to 390 degrees F.
   In a large bowl, add all ingredients except mushrooms and mix till well combined.
   In a baking pan, place the beef mixture.
   With the back of spatula, smooth the surface.
   Top with mushroom slices and gently, press into the meatloaf.
   Drizzle with oil evenly.

2 **Air Frying**. Arrange the pan in the Chefman air fryer basket and cook for about 25 minutes.
   Cut the meatloaf in desires size wedges and serve.

Beef and Broccoli

PREP: 10 MINUTES • COOK TIME: 12 MINUTES • TOTAL: 25 MINUTES
SERVES: 4

Ingredients

1 minced garlic clove
1 sliced ginger root
1 tbsp. olive oil
1 tsp. almond flour
1 tsp. sweetener of choice
1 tsp. low-sodium soy sauce
1/3 C. sherry
2 tsp. sesame oil
1/3 C. oyster sauce
1 pounds of broccoli
¾ pound round steak

Directions:

1 **Preparing the Ingredients.** Remove stems from broccoli and slice into florets. Slice steak into thin strips.
Combine sweetener, soy sauce, sherry, almond flour, sesame oil, and oyster sauce together, stirring till sweetener dissolves. Put strips of steak into the mixture and allow to marinate 45 minutes to 2 hours. Add broccoli and marinated steak to air fryer. Place garlic, ginger, and olive oil on top.
2 **Air Frying.** Set temperature to 400°F, and set time to 12 minutes. Cook 12 minutes at 400 degrees. Serve with cauliflower rice!

PER SERVING: CALORIES: 384; FAT: 16G; PROTEIN:19G; SUGAR:4G

Air Fryer Beef Fajitas

PREP: 5 MINUTES • COOK TIME: 20 MINUTES • TOTAL: 25 MINUTES
SERVES: 6

Ingredients

Beef:
1/8 C. carne asada seasoning
2 pounds beef flap meat
Diet 7-Up
Fajita veggies:
1 tsp. chili powder
1-2 tsp. pepper
1-2 tsp. salt
2 bell peppers, your choice of color
1 onion

Directions:

1 **Preparing the Ingredients.** Slice flap meat into manageable pieces and place into a bowl. Season meat with carne seasoning and pour diet soda over meat. Cover and chill overnight.
Ensure your air fryer is preheated to 380 degrees.
Place a parchment liner into the Chefman air fryer basket and spray with olive oil. Place beef in layers into the basket.
Cook 8-10 minutes, making sure to flip halfway through. Remove and set to the side.
Slice up veggies and spray air fryer basket. Add veggies to the fryer and spray with olive oil.
2 **Air Frying.** Set temperature to 400°F, and set time to 10 minutes. Cook 10 minutes at 400 degrees, shaking 1-2 times during cooking process.
Serve meat and veggies on wheat tortillas and top with favorite keto fillings!

PER SERVING: CALORIES: 412; FAT: 21G; PROTEIN:13G; SUGAR:1G

Coconut Shrimp

PREP: 5 MINUTES • COOK TIME: 10 MINUTES • TOTAL: 15 MINUTES
SERVES: 3

Ingredients
1 C. almond flour
1 C. panko breadcrumbs
1 tbsp. coconut flour
1 C. unsweetened, dried coconut
1 egg white
12 raw large shrimp

Directions:
1 **Preparing the Ingredients.** Put shrimp on paper towels to drain.
   Mix coconut and panko breadcrumbs together. Then mix in coconut flour and almond flour in a different bowl. Set to the side.
   Dip shrimp into flour mixture, then into egg white, and then into coconut mixture. Place into air fryer basket. Repeat with remaining shrimp.
2 **Air Frying.** Set temperature to 350°F, and set time to 10 minutes. Turn halfway through cooking process.

PER SERVING: CALORIES:213; FAT: 8G; PROTEIN:15G; SUGAR:3G

Grilled Salmon

PREP: 5 MINUTES • COOK TIME: 10 MINUTES • TOTAL: 15 MINUTES
SERVES: 3

Ingredients
2 Salmon Fillets
1/2 Tsp Lemon Pepper
1/2 Tsp Garlic Powder
Salt and Pepper
1/3 Cup Soy Sauce
1/3 Cup Sugar
1 Tbsp Olive Oil

Directions:
Preparing the Ingredients. Season salmon fillets with lemon pepper, garlic powder and salt. In a shallow bowl, add a third cup of water and combine the olive oil, soy sauce and sugar. Place salmon the bowl and immerse in the sauce. Cover with cling film and allow to marinate in the refrigerator for at least an hour
1 **Air Frying.** Preheat the Chefman air fryer at 350 degrees.
   Place salmon into the Chefman air fryer and cook for 10 minutes or more until the fish is tender.
   Serve with lemon wedges

Bacon Wrapped Shrimp

PREP: 5 MINUTES • COOK TIME: 5 MINUTES • TOTAL: 10 MINUTES
SERVES: 4

Ingredients

1¼ pound tiger shrimp, peeled and deveined
1 pound bacon

Directions:

1 **Preparing the Ingredients.** Wrap each shrimp with a slice of bacon.
   Refrigerate for about 20 minutes.
   Preheat the Chefman air fryer to 390 degrees F.
2 **Air Frying.** Arrange the shrimp in the Chefman air fryer basket.
   Cook for about 5-7 minutes.

Crispy Paprika Fish Fillets

PREP: 5 MINUTES • COOK TIME: 15 MINUTES • TOTAL: 20 MINUTES
SERVES: 4

Ingredients

1/2 cup seasoned breadcrumbs
1 tablespoon balsamic vinegar
1/2 teaspoon seasoned salt
1 teaspoon paprika
1/2 teaspoon ground black pepper
1 teaspoon celery seed
2 fish fillets, halved
1 egg, beaten

Directions:

1 **Preparing the Ingredients.** Add the breadcrumbs, vinegar, salt, paprika, ground black pepper, and celery seeds to your food processor. Process for about 30 seconds.
   Coat the fish fillets with the beaten egg; then, coat them with the breadcrumbs mixture.
2 **Air Frying.** Cook at 350 degrees F for about 15 minutes.

Air Fryer Salmon

PREP: 5 MINUTES • COOK TIME: 10 MINUTES • TOTAL: 15 MINUTES
SERVES: 2

Ingredients
½ tsp. salt
½ tsp. garlic powder
½ tsp. smoked paprika
Salmon

Directions:
1. **Preparing the Ingredients.** Mix spices together and sprinkle onto salmon. Place seasoned salmon into the Chefman air fryer.
2. **Air Frying.** Close crisping lid. Set temperature to 400°F, and set time to 10 minutes.

PER SERVING: CALORIES: 185; FAT: 11G; PROTEIN:21G; SUGAR:0G

Steamed Salmon & Sauce

PREP: 5 MINUTES • COOK TIME: 10 MINUTES • TOTAL: 15 MINUTES
SERVES: 2

Ingredients
1 cup Water
2 x 6 oz Fresh Salmon
2 Tsp Vegetable Oil
A Pinch of Salt for Each Fish
½ cup Plain Greek Yogurt
½ cup Sour Cream
2 Tbsp Finely Chopped Dill (Keep a bit for garnishing)
A Pinch of Salt to Taste

Directions:
1. **Preparing the Ingredients.** Pour the water into the bottom of the fryer and start heating to 285° F.
Drizzle oil over the fish and spread it. Salt the fish to taste.
2. **Air Frying.** Now pop it into the fryer for 10 min.
In the meantime, mix the yogurt, cream, dill and a bit of salt to make the sauce. When the fish is done, serve with the sauce and garnish with sprigs of dill.

Sweet And Savory Breaded Shrimp

PREP: 5 MINUTES • COOK TIME: 20 MINUTES • TOTAL: 25 MINUTES
SERVES: 2

Ingredients

½ pound of fresh shrimp, peeled from their shells and rinsed
2 raw eggs
½ cup of breadcrumbs (we like Panko, but any brand or home recipe will do)
½ white onion, peeled and rinsed and finely chopped
1 teaspoon of ginger-garlic paste
½ teaspoon of turmeric powder
½ teaspoon of red chili powder
½ teaspoon of cumin powder
½ teaspoon of black pepper powder
½ teaspoon of dry mango powder
Pinch of salt

Directions:

1 **Preparing the Ingredients.** Cover the basket of the Chefman air fryer with a lining of tin foil, leaving the edges uncovered to allow air to circulate through the basket.

Preheat the Chefman air fryer to 350 degrees.

In a large mixing bowl, beat the eggs until fluffy and until the yolks and whites are fully combined.

Dunk all the shrimp in the egg mixture, fully submerging.

In a separate mixing bowl, combine the bread crumbs with all the dry ingredients until evenly blended.

One by one, coat the egg-covered shrimp in the mixed dry ingredients so that fully covered, and place on the foil-lined air-fryer basket.

2 **Air Frying.** Set the air-fryer timer to 20 minutes.

Halfway through the cooking time, shake the handle of the air-fryer so that the breaded shrimp jostles inside and fry-coverage is even.

After 20 minutes, when the fryer shuts off, the shrimp will be perfectly cooked and their breaded crust golden-brown and delicious! Using tongs, remove from the air fryer and set on a serving dish to cool.

Indian Fish Fingers

PREP: 35 MINUTES • COOK TIME: 15 MINUTES • TOTAL: 50 MINUTES
SERVES: 4

Ingredients

1/2 pound fish fillet
1 tablespoon finely chopped fresh mint leaves or any fresh herbs
1/3 cup bread crumbs
1 teaspoon ginger garlic paste or ginger and garlic powders
1 hot green chili finely chopped
1/2 teaspoon paprika
Generous pinch of black pepper
Salt to taste
3/4 tablespoons lemon juice
3/4 teaspoons garam masala powder
1/3 teaspoon rosemary
1 egg

Directions:

1 **Preparing the Ingredients.** Start by removing any skin on the fish, washing, and patting dry. Cut the fish into fingers.
   In a medium bowl mix together all ingredients except for fish, mint, and bread crumbs. Bury the fingers in the mixture and refrigerate for 30 minutes.
   Remove from the bowl from the fridge and mix in mint leaves.
   In a separate bowl beat the egg, pour bread crumbs into a third bowl. Dip the fingers in the egg bowl then toss them in the bread crumbs bowl.
2 **Air Frying.** Cook at 360 degrees for 15 minutes, toss the fingers halfway through.
   PER SERVING: CALORIES: 187; FAT: 7G; PROTEIN:11G; FIBER:1G

Healthy Fish and Chips

PREP: 5 MINUTES • COOK TIME: 15 MINUTES • TOTAL: 20 MINUTES
SERVES: 3

Ingredients

Old Bay seasoning
½ C. panko breadcrumbs
1 egg
2 tbsp. almond flour
4-6 ounce tilapia fillets
Frozen crinkle cut fries

Directions:

1 **Preparing the Ingredients.** Add almond flour to one bowl, beat egg in another bowl, and add panko breadcrumbs to the third bowl, mixed with Old Bay seasoning. Dredge tilapia in flour, then egg, and then breadcrumbs.
   Place coated fish in Chefman air fryer along with fries.
2 **Air Frying**. Set temperature to 390°F, and set time to 15 minutes.

PER SERVING: CALORIES: 219; FAT: 5G; PROTEIN:25G; SUGAR:1G

Quick Paella

PREP: 7 MINUTES • COOK TIME: 15 MINUTES • TOTAL: 22 MINUTES
SERVES: 4

Ingredients

1 (10-ounce) package frozen cooked rice, thawed
1 (6-ounce) jar artichoke hearts, drained and chopped
¼ cup vegetable broth
½ teaspoon turmeric
½ teaspoon dried thyme
1 cup frozen cooked small shrimp
½ cup frozen baby peas
1 tomato, diced

Directions:

1 **Preparing the Ingredients.** In a 6-by-6-by-2-inch pan, combine the rice, artichoke hearts, vegetable broth, turmeric, and thyme, and stir gently.
2 **Air Frying.** Place in the Chefman air fryer and bake for 8 to 9 minutes or until the rice is hot. Remove from the air fryer and gently stir in the shrimp, peas, and tomato. Cook for 5 to 8 minutes or until the shrimp and peas are hot and the paella is bubbling.

PER SERVING: CALORIES: 345; FAT: 1G; PROTEIN:18G; FIBER:4G

Coconut Shrimp

PREP: 15 MINUTES • COOK TIME: 5 MINUTES • TOTAL: 20 MINUTES
SERVES: 4

Ingredients

1 (8-ounce) can crushed pineapple
½ cup sour cream
¼ cup pineapple preserves
2 egg whites
⅔ cup cornstarch
⅔ cup sweetened coconut
1 cup panko bread crumbs
1 pound uncooked large shrimp, thawed if frozen, deveined and shelled
Olive oil for misting

Directions:

1 **Preparing the Ingredients.** Drain the crushed pineapple well, reserving the juice. In a small bowl, combine the pineapple, sour cream, and preserves, and mix well. Set aside. In a shallow bowl, beat the egg whites with 2 tablespoons of the reserved pineapple liquid. Place the cornstarch on a plate. Combine the coconut and bread crumbs on another plate. Dip the shrimp into the cornstarch, shake it off, then dip into the egg white mixture and finally into the coconut mixture. Place the shrimp in the air fryer basket and mist with oil.
2 **Air Frying.** Air-fry for 5 to 7 minutes or until the shrimp are crisp and golden brown

PER SERVING: CALORIES: 524; FAT: 14G; PROTEIN:33G; FIBER:4G

3-Ingredient Air Fryer Catfish

PREP: 5 MINUTES • COOK TIME: 13 MINUTES • TOTAL: 20 MINUTES
SERVES: 4

Ingredients
1 tbsp. chopped parsley
1 tbsp. olive oil
¼ C. seasoned fish fry
4 catfish fillets

Directions:
1 **Preparing the Ingredients.** Ensure your air fryer is preheated to 400 degrees.
Rinse off catfish fillets and pat dry.
Add fish fry seasoning to Ziploc baggie, then catfish. Shake bag and ensure fish gets well coated.
Spray each fillet with olive oil.
Add fillets to air fryer basket.
2 **Air Frying.** Set temperature to 400°F, and set time to 10 minutes.
Cook 10 minutes. Then flip and cook another 2-3 minutes.

PER SERVING: CALORIES: 208; FAT: 5G; PROTEIN:17G; SUGAR:0.5G

Tuna Veggie Stir-Fry

PREP: 5 MINUTES • COOK TIME: 12 MINUTES • TOTAL: 17 MINUTES
SERVES: 4

Ingredients
1 tablespoon olive oil
1 red bell pepper, chopped
1 cup green beans, cut into 2-inch pieces
1 onion, sliced
2 cloves garlic, sliced
2 tablespoons low-sodium soy sauce
1 tablespoon honey
½ pound fresh tuna, cubed

Directions:
1 **Preparing the Ingredients.** In a 6-inch metal bowl, combine the olive oil, pepper, green beans, onion, and garlic.
2 **Air Frying.** Cook in the Chefman air fryer for 4 to 6 minutes, stirring once, until crisp and tender. Add soy sauce, honey, and tuna, and stir. Cook for another 3 to 6 minutes, stirring once, until the tuna is cooked as desired. Tuna can be served rare or medium-rare, or you can cook it until well done.

PER SERVING: CALORIES: 187; FAT: 8G; PROTEIN:17G; FIBER:2G

Salmon Quiche

PREP: 5 MINUTES • COOK TIME: 12 MINUTES • TOTAL: 17 MINUTES
SERVES: 4

Ingredients

5 Ozs Salmon Fillet
1/2 Tbsp Lemon Juice
1/2 Cup Flour
1/4 Cup Butter, melted
2 Eggs and 1 Egg Yolk
3 Tbsps Whipped Cream
Tsps Mustard
Black Pepper to taste
Salt and Pepper
* Quiche Pan

Directions:

1 **Preparing the Ingredients.** Clean and cut the salmon into small cubes.
   Heat the Chefman air fryer to 375 degrees
   Pour the lemon juice over the salmon cubes and allow to marinate for an hour.
   Combine a tablespoon of water with the butter, flour and yolk in a large bowl. Using your hands, knead the mixture until smooth
   On a clean surface, use a rolling pin to form a circle of dough. Place this into the quiche pan, using your fingers to adhere the pastry to the edges
   Whisk the cream, mustard and eggs together. Season with salt and pepper. Add the marinated salmon into the bowl and combine.
   Pour the content of the bowl into the dough lined quiche pan
2 **Air Frying.** Put the pan in the Chefman air fryer tray and cook for 25 minutes until browned and crispy.

Cilantro-Lime Fried Shrimp

PREP: 10 MINUTES • COOK TIME: 10 MINUTES • TOTAL: 20 MINUTES
SERVES: 4

Ingredients

1 pound raw shrimp, peeled and deveined with tails on or off (see Prep tip)
½ cup chopped fresh cilantro
Juice of 1 lime
1 egg
½ cup all-purpose flour
¾ cup bread crumbs
Salt
Pepper
Cooking oil
½ cup cocktail sauce (optional)

Directions:

1 **Preparing the Ingredients.** Place the shrimp in a plastic bag and add the cilantro and lime juice. Seal the bag. Shake to combine. Marinate in the refrigerator for 30 minutes.
   In a small bowl, beat the egg. In another small bowl, place the flour. Place the bread crumbs in a third small bowl, and season with salt and pepper to taste.
   Spray the air fryer basket with cooking oil. Remove the shrimp from the plastic bag. Dip each in the flour, then the egg, and then the bread crumbs.
2 **Air Frying.** Place the shrimp in the Chefman air fryer air fryer. It is okay to stack them. Spray the shrimp with cooking oil. Cook for 4 minutes.
   Open the air fryer and flip the shrimp. I recommend flipping individually instead of shaking to keep the breading intact. Cook for an additional 4 minutes, or until crisp.
   Cool before serving. Serve with cocktail sauce if desired.

PER SERVING: CALORIES: 254; FAT:4G;
PROTEIN:29G; FIBER:1G

Lemony Tuna

**PREP: 10 MINUTES • COOK TIME: 10
MINUTES • TOTAL: 20 MINUTES
SERVES: 4**

Ingredients

2 (6-ounce) cans water packed plain tuna
2 teaspoons Dijon mustard
½ cup breadcrumbs
1 tablespoon fresh lime juice
2 tablespoons fresh parsley, chopped
1 egg
Chefman air fryer of hot sauce
3 tablespoons canola oil
Salt and freshly ground black pepper, to taste

Directions:

1 **Preparing the Ingredients.** Drain most of
   the liquid from the canned tuna.
   In a bowl, add the fish, mustard, crumbs,
   citrus juice, parsley and hot sauce and mix
   till well combined. Add a little canola oil if
   it seems too dry. Add egg, salt and stir to
   combine. Make the patties from tuna
   mixture. Refrigerate the tuna patties for
   about 2 hours.
2 **Air Frying.** Preheat the air fryer to 355
   degrees F. Cook for about 10-12 minutes

Bang Bang Panko Breaded Fried Shrimp

PREP: 5 MINUTES • COOK TIME: 8 MINUTES • TOTAL: 13 MINUTES
SERVES: 4

Ingredients
1 tsp. paprika
Montreal chicken seasoning
¾ C. panko bread crumbs
½ C. almond flour
1 egg white
1 pound raw shrimp (peeled and deveined)

Bang Bang Sauce:
¼ C. sweet chili sauce
2 tbsp. sriracha sauce
1/3 C. plain Greek yogurt

Directions:
1 **Preparing the Ingredients.** Ensure your air fryer is preheated to 400 degrees. Season all shrimp with seasonings. Add flour to one bowl, egg white in another, and breadcrumbs to a third. Dip seasoned shrimp in flour, then egg whites, and then breadcrumbs. Spray coated shrimp with olive oil and add to air fryer basket.
2 **Air Frying**. Set temperature to 400°F, and set time to 4 minutes. Cook 4 minutes, flip, and cook an additional 4 minutes. To make the sauce, mix together all sauce ingredients until smooth.

PER SERVING: CALORIES: 212; CARBS:12; FAT: 1G; PROTEIN:37G; SUGAR:0.5G

Grilled Soy Salmon Fillets

PREP: 5 MINUTES • COOK TIME: 8 MINUTES • TOTAL: 13 MINUTES
SERVES: 4

Ingredients
4 salmon fillets
1/4 teaspoon ground black pepper
1/2 teaspoon cayenne pepper
1/2 teaspoon salt
1 teaspoon onion powder
1 tablespoon fresh lemon juice
1/2 cup soy sauce
1/2 cup water
1 tablespoon honey
2 tablespoons extra-virgin olive oil

Directions:
1 **Preparing the Ingredients.** Firstly, pat the salmon fillets dry using kitchen towels. Season the salmon with black pepper, cayenne pepper, salt, and onion powder.
To make the marinade, combine together the lemon juice, soy sauce, water, honey, and olive oil. Marinate the salmon for at least 2 hours in your refrigerator.
Arrange the fish fillets on a grill basket in your Chefman air fryer fryer.
2 **Air Frying**. Bake at 330 degrees for 8 to 9 minutes, or until salmon fillets are easily flaked with a fork.
Work with batches and serve warm.

Flying Fish

PREP: 5 MINUTES • COOK TIME: 12 MINUTES • TOTAL: 17 MINUTES
SERVES: 6

Ingredients
4 Tbsp Oil
3–4 oz Breadcrumbs
1 Whisked Whole Egg in a Saucer/Soup Plate
4 Fresh Fish Fillets
Fresh Lemon (For serving)

Directions:

1 **Preparing the Ingredients.** Preheat the Chefman air fryer (if necessary) to 350° F. Mix the crumbs and oil until it looks nice and loose.
Dip the fish in the egg and coat lightly, then move on to the crumbs. Make sure the fillet is covered evenly.

2 **Air Frying.** Cook in the Dah air fryer basket for roughly 12 minutes – depending on the size of the fillets you are using.
Serve with fresh lemon & chips to complete the duo.

Pistachio-Crusted Lemon-Garlic Salmon

PREP: 5 MINUTES • COOK TIME: 20 MINUTES • TOTAL: 25 MINUTES
SERVES: 6

Ingredients
4 medium-sized salmon filets
2 raw eggs
3 ounces of melted butter
1 clove of garlic, peeled and finely minced
1 large-sized lemon
1 teaspoon of salt
1 tablespoon of parsley, rinsed, patted dry and chopped
1 teaspoon of dill, rinsed, patted dry and chopped
½ cup of pistachio nuts, shelled and coarsely crushed

Directions:

1 **Preparing the Ingredients.** Cover the basket of the Chefman air fryer with a lining of tin foil, leaving the edges uncovered to allow air to circulate through the basket.
Preheat the Chefman air fryerto 350 degrees.
In a mixing bowl, beat the eggs until fluffy and until the yolks and whites are fully combined.
Add the melted butter, the juice of the lemon, the minced garlic, the parsley and the dill to the beaten eggs, and stir thoroughly.
One by one, dunk the salmon filets into the wet mixture, then roll them in the crushed pistachios, coating completely.
Place the coated salmon fillets in the Chefman air fryer basket.

2 **Air Frying.** Set the Chefman air fryer timer for 10 minutes.

When the air fryer shuts off, after 10 minutes, the salmon will be partly cooked and the crust beginning to crisp. Using tongs, turn each of the fish filets over.

Reset the Chefman air fryer to 350 degrees for another 10 minutes.

After 10 minutes, when the air fryer shuts off, the salmon will be perfectly cooked and the pistachio crust will be toasted and crispy. Using tongs, remove from the Chefman air fryer and serve.

Louisiana Shrimp Po Boy
PREP: 10 MINUTES • COOK TIME: 10 MINUTES • TOTAL: 20 MINUTES
SERVES: 6

Ingredients
1 tsp. creole seasoning
8 slices of tomato
Lettuce leaves
¼ C. buttermilk
½ C. Louisiana Fish Fry
1 pound deveined shrimp
Remoulade sauce:
1 chopped green onion
1 tsp. hot sauce
1 tsp. Dijon mustard
½ tsp. creole seasoning
1 tsp. Worcestershire sauce
Juice of ½ a lemon
½ C. vegan mayo

Directions:
1. **Preparing the Ingredients.** To make the sauce, combine all sauce ingredients until well incorporated. Chill while you cook shrimp.
   Mix seasonings together and liberally season shrimp.
   Add buttermilk to a bowl. Dip each shrimp into milk and place in a Ziploc bag. Chill half an hour to marinate.
   Add fish fry to a bowl. Take shrimp from marinating bag and dip into fish fry, then add to air fryer.
   Ensure your air fryer is preheated to 400 degrees.
   Spray shrimp with olive oil.
2. **Air Frying.** Set temperature to 400°F, and set time to 5 minutes. Cook 5 minutes, flip and then cook another 5 minutes.
   Assemble "Keto" Po Boy by adding sauce to lettuce leaves, along with shrimp and tomato.

Old Bay Crab Cakes

PREP: 10 MINUTES • COOK TIME: 20 MINUTES • TOTAL: 30 MINUTES
SERVES: 4

Ingredients

slices dried bread, crusts removed
Small amount of milk
1 tablespoon mayonnaise
1 tablespoon Worcestershire sauce
1 tablespoon baking powder
1 tablespoon parsley flakes
1 teaspoon Old Bay® Seasoning
1/4 teaspoon salt
1 egg
1 pound lump crabmeat

Directions:

1 **Preparing the Ingredients.** Crush your bread over a large bowl until it is broken down into small pieces. Add milk and stir until bread crumbs are moistened. Mix in mayo and Worcestershire sauce. Add remaining ingredients and mix well. Shape into 4 patties.
2 **Air Frying.** Cook at 360 degrees for 20 minutes, flip half way through.

PER SERVING: CALORIES: 165; CARBS:5.8; FAT: 4.5G; PROTEIN:24G; FIBER:0G

Scallops and Spring Veggies

PREP: 10 MINUTES • COOK TIME: 8 MINUTES • TOTAL: 18 MINUTES

SERVES: 4

Ingredients

½ pound asparagus, ends trimmed, cut into 2-inch pieces
1 cup sugar snap peas
1 pound sea scallops
1 tablespoon lemon juice
2 teaspoons olive oil
½ teaspoon dried thyme
Pinch salt
Freshly ground black pepper

Directions:

1 **Preparing the Ingredients.** Place the asparagus and sugar snap peas in the Chefman air fryer basket.
2 **Air Frying.** Cook for 2 to 3 minutes or until the vegetables are just starting to get tender.
Meanwhile, check the scallops for a small muscle attached to the side, and pull it off and discard.
In a medium bowl, toss the scallops with the lemon juice, olive oil, thyme, salt, and pepper. Place into the Chefman air fryer basket on top of the vegetables.
3 **Air Frying.** Steam for 5 to 7 minutes, tossing the basket once during cooking time, until the scallops are just firm when tested with your finger and are opaque in the center, and the vegetables are tender. Serve immediately.

PER SERVING: CALORIES: 162; CARBS:10G; FAT: 4G; PROTEIN:22G; FIBER:3G

Air Fryer Salmon Patties

PREP: 8 MINUTES • COOK TIME: 7 MINUTES • TOTAL: 15 MINUTES

SERVES: 4

Ingredients

1 tbsp. olive oil
1 tbsp. ghee
¼ tsp. salt
1/8 tsp. pepper
1 egg
1 C. almond flour
1 can wild Alaskan pink salmon

Directions:

1. **Preparing the Ingredients.** Drain can of salmon into a bowl and keep liquid. Discard skin and bones.
Add salt, pepper, and egg to salmon, mixing well with hands to incorporate. Make patties.
Dredge in flour and remaining egg. If it seems dry, spoon reserved salmon liquid from the can onto patties.
2. **Air Frying.** Add patties to the Chefman air fryer. Cook 7 minutes at 378 degrees till golden, making sure to flip once during cooking process.

PER SERVING: CALORIES: 437; CARBS:55; FAT: 12G; PROTEIN:24G; SUGAR:2G

Salmon Noodles

PREP: 5 MINUTES • COOK TIME: 16 MINUTES • TOTAL: 21 MINUTES
SERVES: 4

Ingredients
1 Salmon Fillet
1 Tbsp Teriyaki Marinade
3 ½ Ozs Soba Noodles, cooked and drained
10 Ozs Firm Tofu
7 Ozs Mixed Salad
1 Cup Broccoli
Olive Oil
Salt and Pepper to taste

Directions:
1 **Preparing the Ingredients**. Season the salmon with salt and pepper to taste, then coat with the teriyaki marinate. Set aside for 15 minutes
2 **Air Frying**. Preheat the Chefman air fryer at 350 degrees, then cook the salmon for 8 minutes.
Whilst the Chefman air fryer is cooking the salmon, start slicing the tofu into small cubes.
Next, slice the broccoli into smaller chunks. Drizzle with olive oil.
Once the salmon is cooked, put the broccoli and tofu into the Chefman air fryer tray for 8 minutes.
Plate the salmon and broccoli tofu mixture over the soba noodles. Add the mixed salad to the side and serve

Beer-Battered Fish and Chips

PREP: 5 MINUTES • COOK TIME: 30 MINUTES • TOTAL: 35 MINUTES
SERVES: 4

Ingredients
2 eggs
1 cup malty beer, such as Pabst Blue Ribbon
1 cup all-purpose flour
½ cup cornstarch
1 teaspoon garlic powder
Salt
Pepper
Cooking oil
(4-ounce) cod fillets

Directions:
1 **Preparing the Ingredients**. In a medium bowl, beat the eggs with the beer. In another medium bowl, combine the flour and cornstarch, and season with the garlic powder and salt and pepper to taste.
Spray the Chefman air fryer basket with cooking oil.
Dip each cod fillet in the flour and cornstarch mixture and then in the egg and beer mixture. Dip the cod in the flour and cornstarch a second time.
2 **Air Frying**. Place the cod in the Chefman air fryer. Do not stack. Cook in batches. Spray with cooking oil. Cook for 8 minutes. Open the Chefman air fryer and flip the cod. Cook for an additional 7 minutes.
Remove the cooked cod from the Chefman air fryer, then repeat steps 4 and 5 for the remaining fillets.
Serve with prepared air fried frozen fries. Frozen fries will need to be cooked for 18 to 20 minutes at 400ºF.
Cool before serving.

PER SERVING: CALORIES: 325; CARBS:41; FAT: 4G; PROTEIN:26G; FIBER:1G

Tuna Stuffed Potatoes

PREP: 5 MINUTES • COOK TIME: 30 MINUTES • TOTAL: 35 MINUTES
SERVES: 4

Ingredients
4 starchy potatoes
½ tablespoon olive oil
1 (6-ounce) can tuna, drained
2 tablespoons plain Greek yogurt
1 teaspoon red chili powder
Salt and freshly ground black pepper, to taste
1 scallion, chopped and divided
1 tablespoon capers

Directions:
1. **Preparing the Ingredients**. In a large bowl of water, soak the potatoes for about 30 minutes. Drain well and pat dry with paper towel.
   Preheat the Chefman air fryer to 355 degrees F. Place the potatoes in a fryer basket.
2. **Air Frying**. Cook for about 30 minutes. Meanwhile in a bowl, add tuna, yogurt, red chili powder, salt, black pepper and half of scallion and with a potato masher, mash the mixture completely.
   Remove the potatoes from the Chefman air fryer and place onto a smooth surface.
   Carefully, cut each potato from top side lengthwise.
   With your fingers, press the open side of potato halves slightly. Stuff the potato open portion with tuna mixture evenly.
   Sprinkle with the capers and remaining scallion. Serve immediately.

Fried Calamari

PREP: 8 MINUTES • COOK TIME: 7 MINUTES • TOTAL: 15 MINUTES
SERVES: 6-8

Ingredients
½ tsp. salt
½ tsp. Old Bay seasoning
1/3 C. plain cornmeal
½ C. semolina flour
½ C. almond flour
5-6 C. olive oil
1 ½ pounds baby squid

Directions:
1. **Preparing the Ingredients.** Rinse squid in cold water and slice tentacles, keeping just ¼-inch of the hood in one piece. Combine 1-2 pinches of pepper, salt, Old Bay seasoning, cornmeal, and both flours together. Dredge squid pieces into flour mixture and place into the Chefman air fryer.
2. **Air Frying.** Spray liberally with olive oil. Cook 15 minutes at 345 degrees till coating turns a golden brown.

PER SERVING: CALORIES: 211; CARBS:55; FAT: 6G; PROTEIN:21G; SUGAR:1G

Soy and Ginger Shrimp

PREP: 8 MINUTES • COOK TIME: 10 MINUTES • TOTAL: 15 MINUTES
SERVES: 4

Ingredients

2 tablespoons olive oil
2 tablespoons scallions, finely chopped
2 cloves garlic, chopped
1 teaspoon fresh ginger, grated
1 tablespoon dry white wine
1 tablespoon balsamic vinegar
1/4 cup soy sauce
1 tablespoon sugar
1 pound shrimp
Salt and ground black pepper, to taste

Directions:

1 **Preparing the Ingredients.** To make the marinade, warm the oil in a saucepan; cook all ingredients, except the shrimp, salt, and black pepper. Now, let it cool.
Marinate the shrimp, covered, at least an hour, in the refrigerator.

2 **Air Frying.** After that, bake the shrimp at 350 degrees F for 8 to 10 minutes (depending on the size), turning once or twice. Season prepared shrimp with salt and black pepper and serve right away!

Crispy Cheesy Fish Fingers

PREP: 10 MINUTES • COOK TIME: 20 MINUTES • TOTAL: 30 MINUTES
SERVES: 4

Ingredients

Large cod fish filet, approximately 6-8 ounces, fresh or frozen and thawed, cut into 1 ½-inch strips
2 raw eggs
½ cup of breadcrumbs (we like Panko, but any brand or home recipe will do)
2 tablespoons of shredded or powdered parmesan cheese
1 tablespoons of shredded cheddar cheese
Pinch of salt and pepper

Directions:

1 **Preparing the Ingredients.** Cover the basket of the Chefman air fryer with a lining of tin foil, leaving the edges uncovered to allow air to circulate through the basket.
Preheat the air fryer to 350 degrees.
In a large mixing bowl, beat the eggs until fluffy and until the yolks and whites are fully combined.
Dunk all the fish strips in the beaten eggs, fully submerging.
In a separate mixing bowl, combine the bread crumbs with the parmesan, cheddar, and salt and pepper, until evenly mixed.
One by one, coat the egg-covered fish strips in the mixed dry ingredients so that they're fully covered, and place on the foil-lined Chefman air fryer basket.

2 **Air Frying.** Set the air-fryer timer to 20 minutes.
Halfway through the cooking time, shake the handle of the air-fryer so that the breaded fish jostles inside and fry-coverage is even.
After 20 minutes, when the fryer shuts off, the fish strips will be perfectly cooked and their breaded crust golden-brown and

delicious! Using tongs, remove from the air fryer and set on a serving dish to cool.

Panko-Crusted Tilapia
PREP: 5 MINUTES • COOK TIME: 10 MINUTES • TOTAL: 15 MINUTES SERVES: 3

Ingredients
2 tsp. Italian seasoning
2 tsp. lemon pepper
1/3 C. panko breadcrumbs
1/3 C. egg whites
1/3 C. almond flour
3 tilapia fillets
Olive oil

Directions:
1. **Preparing the Ingredients.** Place panko, egg whites, and flour into separate bowls. Mix lemon pepper and Italian seasoning in with breadcrumbs.
   Pat tilapia fillets dry. Dredge in flour, then egg, then breadcrumb mixture.
2. **Air Frying.** Add to the Chefman air fryer basket and spray lightly with olive oil.
   Cook 10-11 minutes at 400 degrees, making sure to flip halfway through cooking.

PER SERVING: CALORIES: 256; FAT: 9G; PROTEIN:39G; SUGAR:5G

Potato Crusted Salmon

PREP: 10 MINUTES • COOK TIME: 15 MINUTES • TOTAL: 25 MINUTES
SERVES: 4

Ingredients

1 pound salmon, swordfish or arctic char fillets, 3/4 inch thick
1 egg white
2 tablespoons water
1/3 cup dry instant mashed potatoes
2 teaspoons cornstarch
1 teaspoon paprika
1 teaspoon lemon pepper seasoning

Directions:

1. **Preparing the Ingredients.** Remove and skin from the fish and cut it into 4 serving pieces Mix together the egg white and water. Mix together all of the dry ingredients. Dip the filets into the egg white mixture then press into the potato mix to coat evenly.
2. **Air Frying.** In your Chefman air fryer, cook at 360 degrees for 15 minutes, flip the filets halfway through.

PER SERVING: CALORIES:176; FAT: 7G; PROTEIN:23G; :5G

Salmon Croquettes

PREP: 5 MINUTES • COOK TIME: 10 MINUTES • TOTAL: 15 MINUTES
SERVES: 6-8

Ingredients

Panko breadcrumbs
Almond flour
2 egg whites
2 tbsp. chopped chives
2 tbsp. minced garlic cloves
½ C. chopped onion
2/3 C. grated carrots
1 pound chopped salmon fillet

Directions:

1. **Preparing the Ingredients**. Mix together all ingredients minus breadcrumbs, flour, and egg whites.
   Shape mixture into balls. Then coat them in flour, then egg, and then breadcrumbs. Drizzle with olive oil.
2. **Air Frying.** Add coated salmon balls to air fryer and cook 6 minutes at 350 degrees. Shake and cook an additional 4 minutes until golden in color.

PER SERVING: CALORIES: 503; CARBS:61g; FAT: 9G; PROTEIN:5G; SUGAR:4G

Snapper Scampi

PREP: 5 MINUTES • COOK TIME: 10 MINUTES • TOTAL: 15 MINUTES
SERVES: 4

Ingredients

4 (6-ounce) skinless snapper or arctic char fillets
1 tablespoon olive oil
3 tablespoons lemon juice, divided
½ teaspoon dried basil
Pinch salt
Freshly ground black pepper
2 tablespoons butter
cloves garlic, minced

Directions:

1 **Preparing the Ingredients.** Rub the fish fillets with olive oil and 1 tablespoon of the lemon juice. Sprinkle with the basil, salt, and pepper, and place in the Chefman air fryer basket.

2 **Air Frying.** Grill the fish for 7 to 8 minutes or until the fish just flakes when tested with a fork. Remove the fish from the basket and put on a serving plate. Cover to keep warm. In a 6-by-6-by-2-inch pan, combine the butter, remaining 2 tablespoons lemon juice, and garlic. Cook in the Chefman air fryer for 1 to 2 minutes or until the garlic is sizzling. Pour this mixture over the fish and serve.

PER SERVING: CALORIES: 265; CARBS:1g; FAT: 11G; PROTEIN:39G; FIBER:0G

Tha Fish Cakes With Mango Relish

PREP: 5 MINUTES • COOK TIME: 10 MINUTES • TOTAL: 15 MINUTES
SERVES: 4

Ingredients

1 lb White Fish Fillets
3 Tbsps Ground Coconut
1 Ripened Mango
½ Tsps Chili Paste
Tbsps Fresh Parsley
1 Green Onion
1 Lime
1 Tsp Salt
1 Egg

Directions:

1 **Preparing the Ingredients.** To make the relish, peel and dice the mango into cubes. Combine with a half teaspoon of chili paste, a tablespoon of parsley, and the zest and juice of half a lime.
In a food processor, pulse the fish until it forms a smooth texture. Place into a bowl and add the salt, egg, chopped green onion, parsley, two tablespoons of the coconut, and the remainder of the chili paste and lime zest and juice. Combine well
Portion the mixture into 10 equal balls and flatten them into small patties. Pour the reserved tablespoon of coconut onto a dish and roll the patties over to coat.
Preheat the Air Fryer to 390 degrees

2 **Air Frying.** Place the fish cakes into the Chefman air fryer and cook for 8 minutes. They should be crisp and lightly browned when ready
Serve hot with mango relish

Air Fryer Fish Tacos
PREP: 5 MINUTES • COOK TIME: 15 MINUTES • TOTAL: 20 MINUTES SERVES: 4

Ingredients
1 pound cod
1 tbsp. cumin
½ tbsp. chili powder
1 ½ C. almond flour
1 ½ C. coconut flour
10 ounces Mexican beer
2 eggs

Directions:
1. **Preparing the Ingredients.** Whisk beer and eggs together.
   Whisk flours, pepper, salt, cumin, and chili powder together.
   Slice cod into large pieces and coat in egg mixture then flour mixture.
2. **Air Frying**. Spray bottom of your Chefman air fryer basket with olive oil and add coated codpieces. Cook 15 minutes at 375 degrees.
   Serve on lettuce leaves topped with homemade salsa.

PER SERVING: CALORIES: 178; CARBS:61g; FAT:10G; PROTEIN:19G; SUGAR:1G

Firecracker Shrimp
PREP: 10 MINUTES • COOK TIME: 8 MINUTES • TOTAL: 18 MINUTES SERVES: 4

Ingredients
For the shrimp
1 pound raw shrimp, peeled and deveined
Salt
Pepper
1 egg
½ cup all-purpose flour
¾ cup panko bread crumbs
Cooking oil
For the firecracker sauce
⅓ cup sour cream
2 tablespoons Sriracha
¼ cup sweet chili sauce

Directions:
1. **Preparing the Ingredients.** Season the shrimp with salt and pepper to taste. In a small bowl, beat the egg. In another small bowl, place the flour. In a third small bowl, add the panko bread crumbs.
   Spray the Chefman air fryer basket with cooking oil. Dip the shrimp in the flour, then the egg, and then the bread crumbs. Place the shrimp in the Chefman air fryer basket. It is okay to stack them. Spray the shrimp with cooking oil.
2. **Air Frying.** Cook for 4 minutes. Open the Chefman air fryer and flip the shrimp. I recommend flipping individually instead of shaking to keep the breading intact. Cook for an additional 4 minutes or until crisp.
   While the shrimp is cooking, make the firecracker sauce: In a small bowl, combine the sour cream, Sriracha, and sweet chili sauce. Mix well. Serve with the shrimp.

PER SERVING: CALORIES: 266; CARBS:23g; FAT:6G; PROTEIN:27G; FIBER:1G

Sesame Seeds Coated Fish
PREP: 10 MINUTES • COOK TIME: 8 MINUTES • TOTAL: 18 MINUTES
SERVES:5

Ingredients
3 tablespoons plain flour
2 eggs
½ cup sesame seeds, toasted
½ cup breadcrumbs
1/8 teaspoon dried rosemary, crushed
Pinch of salt
Pinch of black pepper
3 tablespoons olive oil
5 frozen fish fillets (white fish of your choice)

Directions:
1   **Preparing the Ingredients.** In a shallow dish, place flour. In a second shallow dish, beat the eggs. In a third shallow dish, add remaining ingredients except fish fillets and mix till a crumbly mixture forms.
Coat the fillets with flour and shake off the excess flour.
Next, dip the fillets in egg.
Then coat the fillets with sesame seeds mixture generously.
Preheat the Chefman air fryer to 390 degrees F.
2   **Air Frying.** Line an Air fryer basket with a piece of foil. Arrange the fillets into prepared basket.
Cook for about 14 minutes, flipping once after 10 minutes.

Bacon Wrapped Scallops

PREP: 5 MINUTES • COOK TIME: 5 MINUTES • TOTAL: 10 MINUTES
SERVES: 4

Ingredients
1 tsp. paprika
1 tsp. lemon pepper
5 slices of center-cut bacon
20 raw sea scallops

Directions:
1. **Preparing the Ingredients.** Rinse and drain scallops, placing on paper towels to soak up excess moisture.
   Cut slices of bacon into 4 pieces.
   Wrap each scallop with a piece of bacon, using toothpicks to secure. Sprinkle wrapped scallops with paprika and lemon pepper.
2. **Air Frying.** Spray air fryer basket with olive oil and add scallops.
   Cook 5-6 minutes at 400 degrees, making sure to flip halfway through.

PER SERVING: CALORIES: 389; CARBS:63g; FAT:17G; PROTEIN:21G; SUGAR:1G

Crispy Paprika Fish Fillets

PREP: 5 MINUTES • COOK TIME: 15 MINUTES • TOTAL: 20 MINUTES
SERVES: 4

Ingredients
1/2 cup seasoned breadcrumbs
1 tablespoon balsamic vinegar
1/2 teaspoon seasoned salt
1 teaspoon paprika
1/2 teaspoon ground black pepper
1 teaspoon celery seed
2 fish fillets, halved
1 egg, beaten

Directions:
1. **Preparing the Ingredients.** Add the breadcrumbs, vinegar, salt, paprika, ground black pepper, and celery seeds to your food processor. Process for about 30 seconds.
   Coat the fish fillets with the beaten egg; then, coat them with the breadcrumbs mixture.
2. **Air Frying.** Cook at 350 degrees F for about 15 minutes.

Parmesan Shrimp

PREP: 5 MINUTES • COOK TIME: 10
MINUTES • TOTAL: 15 MINUTES
SERVES: 4

Ingredients

2 tbsp. olive oil
1 tsp. onion powder
1 tsp. basil
½ tsp. oregano
1 tsp. pepper
2/3 C. grated parmesan cheese
4 minced garlic cloves
pounds of jumbo cooked shrimp
(peeled/deveined)

Directions:

1 **Preparing the Ingredients**. Mix all seasonings together and gently toss shrimp with mixture.
2 **Air Frying.** Spray olive oil into the Chefman air fryer basket and add seasoned shrimp.
Cook 8-10 minutes at 350 degrees.
Squeeze lemon juice over shrimp right before devouring!

PER SERVING: CALORIES: 351; FAT:11G; PROTEIN:19G; SUGAR:1G

Flaky Fish Quesadilla

PREP: 10 MINUTES • COOK TIME: 12
MINUTES • TOTAL: 22 MINUTES
SERVES: 4

Ingredients

Two 6-inch corn or flour tortilla shells
1 medium-sized tilapia fillet, approximately 4 ounces
½ medium-sized lemon, sliced
½ an avocado, peeled, pitted and sliced
1 clove of garlic, peeled and finely minced
Pinch of salt and pepper
½ teaspoon of lemon juice
¼ cup of shredded cheddar cheese
¼ cup of shredded mozzarella cheese

Directions:

1 **Preparing the Ingredients.** Preheat the air fryer to 350 degrees.
In the oven, grill the tilapia with a little salt and lemon slices in foil on high heat for 20 minutes.
Remove fish in foil from the oven, and break the fish meat apart into bite-sized pieces with a fork – it should be flaky and chunky when cooked.
While the fish is cooling, combine the avocado, garlic, salt, pepper, and lemon juice in a small mixing bowl; mash lightly, but don't whip - keep the avocado slightly chunky.
Spread the guacamole on one of the tortillas, then cover with the fish flakes, and then with the cheese. Top with the second tortilla.
Place directly on hot surface of the Chefman air frying basket.
2 **Air Frying.** Set the Chefman air fryer timer for 6 minutes.
After 6 minutes, when the Chefman air fryer shuts off, flip the tortillas onto the other side with a spatula; the cheese

should be melted enough that it won't fall apart.

Reset air fryer to 350 degrees for another 6 minutes.

After 6 minutes, when the air fryer shuts off, the tortillas should be browned and crisp, and the fish, guacamole and cheese will be hot and delicious inside. Remove with spatula and let sit on a serving plate to cool for a few minutes before slicing.

Quick Fried Catfish

PREP: 5 MINUTES • COOK TIME: 15 MINUTES • TOTAL: 20 MINUTES SERVES: 4

Ingredients

3/4 cups Original Bisquick™ mix
1/2 cup yellow cornmeal
1 tablespoon seafood seasoning
4 catfish fillets (4 to 6 ounces each)
1/2 cup ranch dressing
Lemon wedges

Directions:

1 **Preparing the Ingredients.** In a shallow bowl mix together the Bisquick mix, cornmeal, and seafood seasoning. Pat the filets dry, then brush them with ranch dressing.
Press the filets into the Bisquick mix on both sides until the filet is evenly coated.

2 **Air Frying.** Cook in your Chefman air fryer at 360 degrees for 15 minutes, flip the filets halfway through.
Serve with a lemon garnish.

PER SERVING: CALORIES: 372; FAT:16G; PROTEIN:28G; FIBER:1.7G

Honey Glazed Salmon

PREP: 5 MINUTES • COOK TIME: 8 MINUTES • TOTAL: 13 MINUTES
SERVES: 2

Ingredients

1 tsp. water
3 tsp. rice wine vinegar
6 tbsp. low-sodium soy sauce
6 tbsp. raw honey
2 salmon fillets

Directions:

1 **Preparing the Ingredients.** Combine water, vinegar, honey, and soy sauce together. Pour half of this mixture into a bowl.
   Place salmon in one bowl of marinade and let chill 2 hours.
2 **Air Frying.** Ensure your Chefman air fryer is preheated to 356 degrees and add salmon.
   Cook 8 minutes, flipping halfway through. Baste salmon with some of the remaining marinade mixture and cook another 5 minutes.
   To make a sauce to serve salmon with, pour remaining marinade mixture into a saucepan, heating till simmering. Let simmer 2 minutes. Serve drizzled over salmon!

PER SERVING: CALORIES: 348; FAT:12G; PROTEIN:20G; SUGAR:3G

Fish and Chips

PREP: 10 MINUTES • COOK TIME: 20 MINUTES • TOTAL: 30 MINUTES
SERVES: 4

Ingredients

4 (4-ounce) fish fillets
Pinch salt
Freshly ground black pepper
½ teaspoon dried thyme
1 egg white
¾ cup crushed potato chips
2 tablespoons olive oil, divided
3 russet potatoes, peeled and cut into strips

Directions:

1 **Preparing the Ingredients.** Pat the fish fillets dry and sprinkle with salt, pepper, and thyme. Set aside.
   In a shallow bowl, beat the egg white until foamy. In another bowl, combine the potato chips and 1 tablespoon of olive oil and mix until combined.
   Dip the fish fillets into the egg white, then into the crushed potato chip mixture to coat.
   Toss the fresh potato strips with the remaining 1 tablespoon olive oil.
2 **Air Frying.** Use your separator to divide the Chefman air fryer basket in half, then fry the chips and fish. The chips will take about 20 minutes; the fish will take about 10 to 12 minutes to cook.

PER SERVING: CALORIES: 374; FAT:16G; PROTEIN:30G; FIBER:4G

Fish Sandwiches

PREP: 10 MINUTES • COOK TIME: 20 MINUTES • TOTAL: 30 MINUTES
SERVES: 4

Ingredients

lbs White Fish Fillets
1/4 Cup Yellow Cornmeal
1 Tsp Greek Seasoning
Salt and Pepper to taste
2 ½ Cups Plain Flour
2 Tsps Baking Powder
2 Cups Beer
4 Hamburger Buns
Mayonnaise
Lettuce Leaves
1 Tomato, sliced
1 Egg

Directions:

1 **Preparing the Ingredients.** Cut the fish fillets into burger patty sized strips. Season with salt and pepper to desired taste.

   In a medium bowl, mix together the beer, egg, baking powder, plain flour, cornmeal, Greek seasoning and additional salt and pepper

   Heat the Chefman air fryer to 340 degrees Place each seasoned fish strip into the batter, ensuring that it is well coated

2 **Air Frying.** Place battered fish into the Chefman air fryer tray and cook in batches for 6 minutes or until crispy

   Compile the sandwich by topping each bun with mayonnaise, then a lettuce leaf, tomato slices, and finally the cooked fish strip

Crab Cakes

PREP: 5 MINUTES • COOK TIME: 10 MINUTES • TOTAL: 15 MINUTES
SERVES: 4

Ingredients

8 ounces jumbo lump crabmeat
1 tablespoon Old Bay Seasoning
⅓ cup bread crumbs
¼ cup diced red bell pepper
¼ cup diced green bell pepper
1 egg
¼ cup mayonnaise
Juice of ½ lemon
1 teaspoon flour
Cooking oil

Directions:

1 **Preparing the Ingredients.** In a large bowl, combine the crabmeat, Old Bay Seasoning, bread crumbs, red bell pepper, green bell pepper, egg, mayo, and lemon juice. Mix gently to combine.

   Form the mixture into 4 patties. Sprinkle ¼ teaspoon of flour on top of each patty.

2 **Air Frying.** Place the crab cakes in the Chefman air fryer. Spray them with cooking oil. Cook for 10 minutes.

   Serve.

Crispy Air Fried Sushi Roll

PREP: 10 MINUTES • COOK TIME: 5 MINUTES • TOTAL: 15 MINUTES
SERVES: 12

PER SERVING: CALORIES: 267; FAT:13G; PROTEIN:6G; SUGAR:3G

Ingredients
Kale Salad:
1 tbsp. sesame seeds
¾ tsp. soy sauce
¼ tsp. ginger
1/8 tsp. garlic powder
¾ tsp. toasted sesame oil
½ tsp. rice vinegar
1 ½ C. chopped kale
Sushi Rolls:
½ of a sliced avocado
3 sheets of sushi nori
1 batch cauliflower rice
Sriracha Mayo:
Sriracha sauce
¼ C. vegan mayo
Coating:

½ C. panko breadcrumbs

Directions:
1 **Preparing the Ingredients.** Combine all of kale salad ingredients together, tossing well. Set to the side.
Lay out a sheet of nori and spread a handful of rice on. Then place 2-3 tbsp. of kale salad over rice, followed by avocado. Roll up sushi.
To make mayo, whisk mayo ingredients together until smooth.
Add breadcrumbs to a bowl.
2 **Air Frying.** Coat sushi rolls in crumbs till coated and add to the Chefman air fryer. Cook rolls 10 minutes at 390 degrees, shaking gently at 5 minutes.
Slice each roll into 6-8 pieces and enjoy!

Sweet Recipes

Perfect Cinnamon Toast

PREP: 10 MINUTES • COOK TIME: 5 MINUTES • TOTAL: 15 MINUTES
SERVES: 6

Ingredients

2 tsp. pepper
1 ½ tsp. vanilla extract
1 ½ tsp. cinnamon
½ C. sweetener of choice
1 C. coconut oil
12 slices whole wheat bread

Directions:

1 **Preparing the Ingredients.** Melt coconut oil and mix with sweetener until dissolved. Mix in remaining ingredients minus bread till incorporated.
Spread mixture onto bread, covering all area.
2 **Air Frying.** Place coated pieces of bread in your Chefman air fryer.
Cook 5 minutes at 400 degrees.
Remove and cut diagonally. Enjoy!

PER SERVING: CALORIES: 124; FAT:2G; PROTEIN:0G; SUGAR:4G

Easy Baked Chocolate Mug Cake

PREP: 5 MINUTES • COOK TIME: 15 MINUTES • TOTAL: 20 MINUTES
SERVES: 3

Ingredients

½ cup cocoa powder
½ cup stevia powder
1 cup coconut cream
1 package cream cheese, room temperature
1 tablespoon vanilla extract
3 tablespoons butter

Directions:

1 **Preparing the Ingredients.** Preheat the Chefman air fryer for 5 minutes.
2 In a mixing bowl, combine all ingredients.
3 Use a hand mixer to mix everything until fluffy.
4 Pour into greased mugs.
5 Place the mugs in the fryer basket.
6 **Air Frying.** Bake for 15 minutes at 350°F.
7 Place in the fridge to chill before serving.

PER SERVING: CALORIES: 744; FAT:69.7G; PROTEIN:13.9G; SUGAR:4G

Angel Food Cake

PREP: 5 MINUTES • COOK TIME: 30 MINUTES • TOTAL: 35 MINUTES SERVES: 12

Ingredients

¼ cup butter, melted
1 cup powdered erythritol
1 teaspoon strawberry extract
12 egg whites
2 teaspoons cream of tartar
A pinch of salt

Directions:

1 **Preparing the Ingredients.** Preheat the Chefman air fryer for 5 minutes.
Mix the egg whites and cream of tartar.
Use a hand mixer and whisk until white and fluffy.
Add the rest of the ingredients except for the butter and whisk for another minute.
Pour into a baking dish.
2 **Air Frying**. Place in the air fryer basket and cook for 30 minutes at 400°F or if a toothpick inserted in the middle comes out clean.
Drizzle with melted butter once cooled.

PER SERVING: CALORIES: 65; FAT:5G; PROTEIN:3.1G; FIBER:1G

Fried Peaches

PREP: 2 HOURS 10 MINUTES • COOK TIME: 15 MINUTES • TOTAL: 15 MINUTES SERVES: 4

Ingredients

4 ripe peaches (1/2 a peach = 1 serving)
1 1/2 cups flour
Salt
2 egg yolks
3/4 cups cold water
1 1/2 tablespoons olive oil
2 tablespoons brandy
4 egg whites
Cinnamon/sugar mix

Directions:

1 **Preparing the Ingredients.** Mix flour, egg yolks, and salt in a mixing bowl. Slowly mix in water, then add brandy. Set the mixture aside for 2 hours and go do something for 1 hour 45 minutes.
Boil a large pot of water and cut and X at the bottom of each peach. While the water boils fill another large bowl with water and ice. Boil each peach for about a minute, then plunge it in the ice bath. Now the peels should basically fall off the peach. Beat the egg whites and mix into the batter mix. Dip each peach in the mix to coat.
2 **Air Frying.** Cook at 360 degrees for 10 Minutes.
Prepare a plate with cinnamon/sugar mix, roll peaches in mix and serve.

PER SERVING: CALORIES: 306; FAT:3G; PROTEIN:10G; FIBER:2.7G

Apple Dumplings
PREP: 10 MINUTES • COOK TIME: 25 MINUTES • TOTAL: 35 MINUTES
SERVES: 4

Ingredients
2 tbsp. melted coconut oil
2 puff pastry sheets
1 tbsp. brown sugar
2 tbsp. raisins
2 small apples of choice

Directions:
1 **Preparing the Ingredients.** Ensure your air fryer is preheated to 356 degrees.
   Core and peel apples and mix with raisins and sugar.
   Place a bit of apple mixture into puff pastry sheets and brush sides with melted coconut oil.
2 **Air Frying.** Place into the Chefman air fryer. Cook 25 minutes, turning halfway through. Will be golden when done.

PER SERVING: CALORIES: 367; FAT:7G; PROTEIN:2G; SUGAR:5G

Apple Pie in Air Fryer
PREP: 5 MINUTES • COOK TIME: 35 MINUTES • TOTAL: 40 MINUTES
SERVES: 4

Ingredients
½ teaspoon vanilla extract
1 beaten egg
1 large apple, chopped
1 Pillsbury Refrigerator pie crust
1 tablespoon butter
1 tablespoon ground cinnamon
1 tablespoon raw sugar
2 tablespoon sugar
2 teaspoons lemon juice
Baking spray

Directions:
1 **Preparing the Ingredients**. Lightly grease baking pan of air fryer with cooking spray. Spread pie crust on bottom of pan up to the sides.
   In a bowl, mix vanilla, sugar, cinnamon, lemon juice, and apples. Pour on top of pie crust. Top apples with butter slices.
   Cover apples with the other pie crust. Pierce with knife the tops of pie.
   Spread beaten egg on top of crust and sprinkle sugar.
   Cover with foil.
2 **Air Frying.** For 25 minutes, cook on 390°F. Remove foil cook for 10 minutes at 330oF until tops are browned.
   Serve and enjoy.

PER SERVING: CALORIES: 372; FAT:19G; PROTEIN:4.2G; SUGAR:5G

Raspberry Cream Rol-Ups

PREP: 10 MINUTES • COOK TIME: 25 MINUTES • TOTAL: 35 MINUTES
SERVES: 4

Ingredients

1 cup of fresh raspberries, rinsed and patted dry
½ cup of cream cheese, softened to room temperature
¼ cup of brown sugar
¼ cup of sweetened condensed milk
1 egg
1 teaspoon of corn starch
6 spring roll wrappers (any brand will do, we like Blue Dragon or Tasty Joy, both available through Target or Walmart, or any large grocery chain)
¼ cup of water

Directions:

1 **Preparing the Ingredients.** Cover the basket of the Chefman air fryer with a lining of tin foil, leaving the edges uncovered to allow air to circulate through the basket. Preheat the Chefman air fryer to 350 degrees.

    In a mixing bowl, combine the cream cheese, brown sugar, condensed milk, cornstarch, and egg. Beat or whip thoroughly, until all ingredients are completely mixed and fluffy, thick and stiff.

    Spoon even amounts of the creamy filling into each spring roll wrapper, then top each dollop of filling with several raspberries.

    Roll up the wraps around the creamy raspberry filling, and seal the seams with a few dabs of water.

    Place each roll on the foil-lined Chefman air fryer basket, seams facing down.

2 **Air Frying.** Set the Chefman air fryer timer to 10 minutes. During cooking, shake the handle of the fryer basket to ensure a nice even surface crisp.

After 10 minutes, when the Chefman air fryer shuts off, the spring rolls should be golden brown and perfect on the outside, while the raspberries and cream filling will have cooked together in a glorious fusion. Remove with tongs and serve hot or cold.

Air Fryer Chocolate Cake

PREP: 5 MINUTES • COOK TIME: 35 MINUTES • TOTAL: 40 MINUTES
SERVES: 8-10

Ingredients
½ C. hot water
1 tsp. vanilla
¼ C. olive oil
½ C. almond milk
1 egg
½ tsp. salt
¾ tsp. baking soda
¾ tsp. baking powder
½ C. unsweetened cocoa powder
2 C. almond flour
1 C. brown sugar

Directions:
1 **Preparing the Ingredients.** Preheat your air fryer to 356 degrees.
   Stir all dry ingredients together. Then stir in wet ingredients. Add hot water last. The batter will be thin, no worries.
2 **Air Frying.** Pour cake batter into a pan that fits into the fryer. Cover with foil and poke holes into the foil.
   Bake 35 minutes.
   Discard foil and then bake another 10 minutes.

PER SERVING: CALORIES: 378; FAT:9G; PROTEIN:4G; SUGAR:5G

Banana-Choco Brownies

PREP: 5 MINUTES • COOK TIME: 30 MINUTES • TOTAL: 35 MINUTES
SERVES: 12

Ingredients
2 cups almond flour
2 teaspoons baking powder
½ teaspoon baking powder
½ teaspoon baking soda
½ teaspoon salt
1 over-ripe banana
3 large eggs
½ teaspoon stevia powder
¼ cup coconut oil
1 tablespoon vinegar
1/3 cup almond flour
1/3 cup cocoa powder

Directions:
1 **Preparing the Ingredients.** Preheat the Chefman air fryer for 5 minutes.
   Combine all ingredients in a food processor and pulse until well-combined. Pour into a baking dish that will fit in the air fryer.
2 **Air Frying.** Place in the air fryer basket and cook for 30 minutes at 350°F or if a toothpick inserted in the middle comes out clean.

PER SERVING: CALORIES: 75; FAT:6.5G; PROTEIN:1.7G; SUGAR:2G

Chocolate Donuts

PREP: 5 MINUTES • COOK TIME: 20 MINUTES • TOTAL: 25 MINUTES
SERVES: 8-10

Ingredients
(8-ounce) can jumbo biscuits
Cooking oil
Chocolate sauce, such as Hershey's

Directions:
1 **Preparing the Ingredients**. Separate the biscuit dough into 8 biscuits and place them on a flat work surface. Use a small circle cookie cutter or a biscuit cutter to cut a hole in the center of each biscuit. You can also cut the holes using a knife. Spray the Chefman air fryer basket with cooking oil.
2 **Air Frying.** Place 4 donuts in the air fryer. Do not stack. Spray with cooking oil. Cook for 4 minutes.
Open the air fryer and flip the donuts. Cook for an additional 4 minutes.
Remove the cooked donuts from the air fryer, then repeat steps 3 and 4 for the remaining 4 donuts.
Drizzle chocolate sauce over the donuts and enjoy while warm.

PER SERVING: CALORIES: 181; FAT:98G; PROTEIN:3G; FIBER:1G

Easy Air Fryer Donuts

PREP: 5 MINUTES • COOK TIME: 5 MINUTES • TOTAL: 10 MINUTES
SERVES: 8

Ingredients
Pinch of allspice
4 tbsp. dark brown sugar
½ - 1 tsp. cinnamon
1/3 C. granulated sweetener
3 tbsp. melted coconut oil
1 can of biscuits

Directions:
1 **Preparing the Ingredients.** Mix allspice, sugar, sweetener, and cinnamon together. Take out biscuits from can and with a circle cookie cutter, cut holes from centers and place into air fryer.
2 **Air Frying.** Cook 5 minutes at 350 degrees. As batches are cooked, use a brush to coat with melted coconut oil and dip each into sugar mixture.
Serve warm!

PER SERVING: CALORIES: 209; FAT:4G; PROTEIN:0G; SUGAR:3G

Chocolate Soufflé for Two

PREP: 5 MINUTES • COOK TIME: 14 MINUTES • TOTAL: 19 MINUTES SERVES: 2

Ingredients

2 tbsp. almond flour
½ tsp. vanilla
3 tbsp. sweetener
2 separated eggs
¼ C. melted coconut oil
3 ounces of semi-sweet chocolate, chopped

Directions:

1 **Preparing the Ingredients.** Brush coconut oil and sweetener onto ramekins. Melt coconut oil and chocolate together. Beat egg yolks well, adding vanilla and sweetener. Stir in flour and ensure there are no lumps.
Preheat fryer to 330 degrees.
Whisk egg whites till they reach peak state and fold them into chocolate mixture.
Pour batter into ramekins and place into the fryer.

2 **Air Frying.** Cook 14 minutes.
Serve with powdered sugar dusted on top.

PER SERVING: CALORIES: 238; FAT:6G; PROTEIN:1G; SUGAR:4G

Fried Bananas with Chocolate Sauce

PREP: 10 MINUTES • COOK TIME: 10 MINUTES • TOTAL: 20 MINUTES SERVES: 2

Ingredients

1 large egg
¼ cup cornstarch
¼ cup plain bread crumbs
3 bananas, halved crosswise
Cooking oil
Chocolate sauce (see Ingredient tip)

Directions:

1 **Preparing the Ingredients.** In a small bowl, beat the egg. In another bowl, place the cornstarch. Place the bread crumbs in a third bowl. Dip the bananas in the cornstarch, then the egg, and then the bread crumbs.
Spray the air fryer basket with cooking oil. Place the bananas in the basket and spray them with cooking oil.

2 **Air Frying.** Cook for 5 minutes. Open the air fryer and flip the bananas. Cook for an additional 2 minutes. Transfer the bananas to plates.
Drizzle the chocolate sauce over the bananas, and serve.
You can make your own chocolate sauce using 2 tablespoons milk and ¼ cup chocolate chips. Heat a saucepan over medium-high heat. Add the milk and stir for 1 to 2 minutes. Add the chocolate chips. Stir for 2 minutes, or until the chocolate has melted.

PER SERVING: CALORIES: 203; FAT:6G; PROTEIN:3G; FIBER:3G

Apple Hand Pies

PREP: 5 MINUTES • COOK TIME: 8 MINUTES • TOTAL: 13 MINUTES
SERVES: 6

Ingredients
15-ounces no-sugar-added apple pie filling
1 store-bought crust

Directions:
1 **Preparing the Ingredients.** Lay out pie crust and slice into equal-sized squares. Place 2 tbsp. filling into each square and seal crust with a fork.
2 **Air Frying.** Place into the Chefman air fryer air fryer. Cook 8 minutes at 390 degrees until golden in color.

PER SERVING: CALORIES: 278; FAT:10G; PROTEIN:5G; SUGAR:4G

Chocolaty Banana Muffins

PREP: 5 MINUTES • COOK TIME: 25 MINUTES • TOTAL: 35 MINUTES
SERVES: 12

Ingredients
¾ cup whole wheat flour
¾ cup plain flour
¼ cup cocoa powder
¼ teaspoon baking powder
1 teaspoon baking soda
¼ teaspoon salt
2 large bananas, peeled and mashed
1 cup sugar
1/3 cup canola oil
1 egg
½ teaspoon vanilla essence
1 cup mini chocolate chips

Directions:
1 **Preparing the Ingredients.** In a large bowl, mix together flour, cocoa powder, baking powder, baking soda and salt.
   In another bowl, add bananas, sugar, oil, egg and vanilla extract and beat till well combined.
   Slowly, add flour mixture in egg mixture and mix till just combined.
   Fold in chocolate chips.
   Preheat the Chefman air fryer to 345 degrees F. Grease 12 muffin molds.
2 **Air Frying.** Transfer the mixture into prepared muffin molds evenly and cook for about 20-25 minutes or till a toothpick inserted in the center comes out clean.
   Remove the muffin molds from Air fryer and keep on wire rack to cool for about 10 minutes. Carefully turn on a wire rack to cool completely before serving.

Blueberry Lemon Muffins

PREP: 5 MINUTES • COOK TIME: 10 MINUTES • TOTAL: 15 MINUTES SERVES: 12

Ingredients

1 tsp. vanilla
Juice and zest of 1 lemon
2 eggs
1 C. blueberries
½ C. cream
¼ C. avocado oil
½ C. monk fruit
2 ½ C. almond flour

Directions:

1 **Preparing the Ingredients**. Mix monk fruit and flour together.
   In another bowl, mix vanilla, egg, lemon juice, and cream together. Add mixtures together and blend well.
   Spoon batter into cupcake holders.
2 **Air Frying**. Place in air fryer. Bake 10 minutes at 320 degrees, checking at 6 minutes to ensure you don't overbake them.

PER SERVING: CALORIES: 317; FAT:11G; PROTEIN:3G; SUGAR:5G

Sweet Cream Cheese Wontons

PREP: 5 MINUTES • COOK TIME: 5 MINUTES • TOTAL: 10 MINUTES SERVES: 16

Ingredients

1 egg mixed with a bit of water
Wonton wrappers
½ C. powdered erythritol
8 ounces softened cream cheese
Olive oil

Directions:

1 **Preparing the Ingredients.** Mix sweetener and cream cheese together.
   Lay out 4 wontons at a time and cover with a dish towel to prevent drying out.
   Place ½ of a teaspoon of cream cheese mixture into each wrapper.
   Dip finger into egg/water mixture and fold diagonally to form a triangle. Seal edges well.
   Repeat with remaining ingredients.
2 **Air Frying.** Place filled wontons into the Chefman air fryer and cook 5 minutes at 400 degrees, shaking halfway through cooking.

PER SERVING: CALORIES: 303; FAT:3G; PROTEIN:0.5G; SUGAR:4G

Air Fryer Cinnamon Rolls
PREP: 15 MINUTES • COOK TIME: 5
MINUTES • TOTAL: 15 MINUTES
SERVES: 8

Ingredients
1 ½ tbsp. cinnamon
¾ C. brown sugar
¼ C. melted coconut oil
1 pound frozen bread dough, thawed
Glaze:
½ tsp. vanilla
1 ¼ C. powdered erythritol
2 tbsp. softened ghee
3   ounces softened cream cheese

Directions:
1   **Preparing the Ingredients.** Lay out bread
    dough and roll out into a rectangle. Brush
    melted ghee over dough and leave a 1-inch
    border along edges.
    Mix cinnamon and sweetener together
    and then sprinkle over dough.
    Roll dough tightly and slice into 8 pieces.
    Let sit 1-2 hours to rise.
    To make the glaze, simply mix ingredients
    together till smooth.
2   **Air Frying.** Once rolls rise, place into air
    fryer and cook 5 minutes at 350 degrees.
    Serve rolls drizzled in cream cheese glaze.
    Enjoy!

PER SERVING: CALORIES: 390; FAT:8G;
PROTEIN:1G; SUGAR:7G

Bread Pudding with Cranberry
PREP: 5 MINUTES • COOK TIME: 45
MINUTES • TOTAL: 50 MINUTES
SERVES: 4

Ingredients
1-1/2 cups milk
2-1/2 eggs
1/2 cup cranberries1 teaspoon butter
1/4 cup and 2 tablespoons white sugar
1/4 cup golden raisins
1/8 teaspoon ground cinnamon
3/4 cup heavy whipping cream
3/4 teaspoon lemon zest
3/4 teaspoon kosher salt
3/4 French baguettes, cut into 2-inch slices
3/8 vanilla bean, split and seeds scraped
away

Directions:
1   **Preparing the Ingredients.** Lightly
    grease baking pan of air fryer with cooking
    spray. Spread baguette slices, cranberries,
    and raisins.
    In blender, blend well vanilla bean,
    cinnamon, salt, lemon zest, eggs, sugar,
    and cream. Pour over baguette slices. Let it
    soak for an hour.
    Cover pan with foil.
2   **Air Frying** For 35 minutes, cook on 330°F.
    Let it rest for 10 minutes.
    Serve and enjoy.

PER SERVING: CALORIES: 581; FAT:23.8G;
PROTEIN:15.8G; SUGAR:7G

Black and White Brownies
PREP: 10 MINUTES • COOK TIME: 20 MINUTES • TOTAL: 30 MINUTES
SERVES: 8

Ingredients
1 egg
¼ cup brown sugar
2 tablespoons white sugar
2 tablespoons safflower oil
1 teaspoon vanilla
¼ cup cocoa powder
⅓ cup all-purpose flour
¼ cup white chocolate chips
Nonstick baking spray with flour

Directions:
1 **Preparing the Ingredients.** In a medium bowl, beat the egg with the brown sugar and white sugar. Beat in the oil and vanilla. Add the cocoa powder and flour, and stir just until combined. Fold in the white chocolate chips.
   Spray a 6-by-6-by-2-inch baking pan with nonstick spray. Spoon the brownie batter into the pan.
2 **Air Frying.** Bake for 20 minutes or until the brownies are set when lightly touched with a finger. Let cool for 30 minutes before slicing to serve.

PER SERVING: CALORIES: 81; FAT:4G; PROTEIN:1G; FIBER:1G

French Toast Bites
PREP: 5 MINUTES • COOK TIME: 15 MINUTES • TOTAL: 20 MINUTES
SERVES: 8

Ingredients
Almond milk
Cinnamon
Sweetener
3 eggs
4 pieces wheat bread

Directions:
1 **Preparing the Ingredients.** Preheat the Chefman air fryer to 360 degrees.
   Whisk eggs and thin out with almond milk.
   Mix 1/3 cup of sweetener with lots of cinnamon.
   Tear bread in half, ball up pieces and press together to form a ball.
   Soak bread balls in egg and then roll into cinnamon sugar, making sure to thoroughly coat.
2 **Air Frying.** Place coated bread balls into the Chefman air fryer and bake 15 minutes.

PER SERVING: CALORIES: 289; FAT:11G; PROTEIN:0G; SUGAR:4G

Baked Apple

PREP: 5 MINUTES • COOK TIME: 20
MINUTES • TOTAL: 25 MINUTES
SERVES: 4

Ingredients
¼ C. water
¼ tsp. nutmeg
¼ tsp. cinnamon
1 ½ tsp. melted ghee
2 tbsp. raisins
2 tbsp. chopped walnuts
1 medium apple

Directions:
1 **Preparing the Ingredients.** Preheat your air fryer to 350 degrees.
   Slice apple in half and discard some of the flesh from the center.
   Place into frying pan.
   Mix remaining ingredients together except water. Spoon mixture to the middle of apple halves.
   Pour water over filled apples.
2 **Air Frying.** Place pan with apple halves into the Chefman air fryer, bake 20 minutes.

PER SERVING: CALORIES: 199; FAT:9G;
PROTEIN:1G; SUGAR:3G

Coffee And Blueberry Cake

PREP: 5 MINUTES • COOK TIME: 35
MINUTES • TOTAL: 40 MINUTES
SERVES: 6

Ingredients
1 cup white sugar
1 egg
1/2 cup butter, softened
1/2 cup fresh or frozen blueberries
1/2 cup sour cream
1/2 teaspoon baking powder
1/2 teaspoon ground cinnamon
1/2 teaspoon vanilla extract
1/4 cup brown sugar
1/4 cup chopped pecans
1/8 teaspoon salt
1-1/2 teaspoons confectioners' sugar for dusting
3/4 cup and 1 tablespoon all-purpose flour

Directions:
1 **Preparing the Ingredients.** In a small bowl, whisk well pecans, cinnamon, and brown sugar.
   In a blender, blend well all wet Ingredients. Add dry Ingredients except for confectioner's sugar and blueberries. Blend well until smooth and creamy.
   Lightly grease baking pan of air fryer with cooking spray.
   Pour half of batter in pan. Sprinkle half of pecan mixture on top. Pour the remaining batter. And then topped with remaining pecan mixture.
   Cover pan with foil.
2 **Air Frying.** For 35 minutes, cook on 330°F. Serve and enjoy with a dusting of confectioner's sugar.

PER SERVING: CALORIES: 471; FAT:24G;
PROTEIN:4.1G; SUGAR:6G

Cinnamon Sugar Roasted Chickpeas

PREP: 5 MINUTES • COOK TIME: 10 MINUTES • TOTAL: 15 MINUTES
SERVES: 2

Ingredients

1 tbsp. sweetener
1 tbsp. cinnamon
1 C. chickpeas

Directions:

1 **Preparing the Ingredients.** Preheat air fryer to 390 degrees.
Rinse and drain chickpeas.
Mix all ingredients together and add to air fryer.
2 **Air Frying.** Cook 10 minutes.

PER SERVING: CALORIES: 111; FAT:19G; PROTEIN:16G; SUGAR:5G

Cherry-Choco Bars

PREP: 5 MINUTES • COOK TIME: 15 MINUTES • TOTAL: 20 MINUTES
SERVES: 8

Ingredients

¼ teaspoon salt
½ cup almonds, sliced
½ cup chia seeds
½ cup dark chocolate, chopped
½ cup dried cherries, chopped
½ cup prunes, pureed
½ cup quinoa, cooked
¾ cup almond butter
1/3 cup honey
2 cups old-fashioned oats
2 tablespoon coconut oil

Directions:

1 **Preparing the Ingredients.** Preheat the air fryer to 375°F.
In a mixing bowl, combine the oats, quinoa, chia seeds, almond, cherries, and chocolate.
In a saucepan, heat the almond butter, honey, and coconut oil.
Pour the butter mixture over the dry mixture. Add salt and prunes.
Mix until well combined.
Pour over a baking dish that can fit inside the air fryer.
2 **Air Frying.** Cook for 15 minutes.
Let it cool for an hour before slicing into bars.

PER SERVING: CALORIES: 321; FAT:17G; PROTEIN:7G; SUGAR:5G

Cinnamon Fried Bananas

PREP: 5 MINUTES • COOK TIME: 10 MINUTES • TOTAL: 15 MINUTES
SERVES: 2-3

Ingredients
1 C. panko breadcrumbs
3 tbsp. cinnamon
½ C. almond flour
3 egg whites
8 ripe bananas
3 tbsp. vegan coconut oil

Directions:
1 **Preparing the Ingredients**. Heat coconut oil and add breadcrumbs. Mix around 2-3 minutes until golden. Pour into bowl.
Peel and cut bananas in half. Roll each bananas half into flour, eggs, and crumb mixture.
2 **Air Frying.** Place into the Chefman air fryer. Cook 10 minutes at 280 degrees.
A great addition to a healthy banana split!

PER SERVING: CALORIES: 219; FAT:10G; PROTEIN:3G; SUGAR:5G

Coconutty Lemon Bars

PREP: 5 MINUTES • COOK TIME: 25 MINUTES • TOTAL: 30 MINUTES
SERVES: 12

Ingredients
¼ cup cashew
¼ cup fresh lemon juice, freshly squeezed
¾ cup coconut milk
¾ cup erythritol
1 cup desiccated coconut
1 teaspoon baking powder
2 eggs, beaten
2 tablespoons coconut oil
A Chefman air fryer of salt

Directions:
1. **Preparing the Ingredients.** Preheat the air fryer for 5 minutes. In a mixing bowl, combine all ingredients. Use a hand mixer to mix everything. Pour into a baking dish that will fit in the air fryer.
2. **Air Frying.** Bake for 25 minutes at 350°F or until a toothpick inserted in the middle comes out clean.

PER SERVING: CALORIES: 118; FAT:10G; PROTEIN:2.6G; SUGAR:5G

To survive, we need to eat. As a result, food has turned into a symbol of loving, nurturing and sharing with one another. Recording, collecting, sharing and remembering the recipes that have been passed to you by your family is a great way to immortalize and honor your family. It is these traditions that carve out your individual personality. You will not just be honoring your family tradition by cooking these recipes, but they will also inspire you to create your own variations, which you can then pass on to your children's.

The recipes are just passed on to everyone, and nobody actually possesses them. I too love sharing recipes. The collection is vibrant and rich as a number of home cooks have offered their inputs to ensure that all of us can cook delicious meals at our home. I am thankful to each one of you who has contributed to this book and has allowed their traditions to pass on and grow with others. You guys are wonderful!

I am also thankful to the cooks who have evaluated all these recipes. You're, as well as, the comments that came from your family members and friends were invaluable.

If you have the time and inclination, please consider leaving a short review wherever you can, we would love to learn more about your opinion.

https://www.amazon.com/review/review-your-purchases/

Deborah is a New York-based food writer, experienced chef. She loves sharing Easy, Delicious and Healthy recipes, especially the delicious and healthy meals that can be prepared using her Air fryer. Deborah is a passionate advocate for the health benefits of a low-carb lifestyle. When she's not cooking, Deborah enjoys spending time with her husband and her kids, gardening and traveling.

Made in the USA
Coppell, TX
09 July 2020